OREGON
BUCKET LIST

*Set Off on **120 Epic Adventures** and Discover Incredible Destinations to Live Out Your Dreams While Creating Unforgettable Memories that Will Last a Lifetime.*

(Online Digital MAP included - access it through the link provided in the MAP Chapter of this book)

BeCrePress Travel

table of contents

TABLE OF CONTENTS

OREGON BUCKET LIST

OREGON BUCKET LIST

OREGON BUCKET LIST

INTRODUCTION

Welcome to a journey that promises not just sights, but transformative experiences—welcome to Oregon Bucket List: Set Off on 120 Epic Adventures and Discover Incredible Destinations to Live Out Your Dreams While Creating Unforgettable Memories That Will Last a Lifetime. As you turn these pages, you're not merely planning trips; you're setting the stage for adventures that will etch themselves into your memory, crafting stories you'll recount for years to come.

Oregon, with its breathtaking landscapes, rich history, and vibrant culture, is more than a destination; it's a call to the heart of every explorer. From the rugged cliffs of the coastline to the serene heights of its mountain ranges, every corner of Oregon offers a unique story, waiting for you to become part of its narrative.

In this guide, each of the 120 destinations is an invitation to experience Oregon's magnificent diversity. You will find detailed descriptions that not only paint a vivid picture of each location but also ignite your imagination. For ease and convenience, every entry includes the destination's address and the nearest city, giving you a clear sense of where each adventure lies in relation to larger urban centers.

Further enriching your journey, the exact GPS coordinates are provided for precision-led travel—ready to be plugged into your device and lead the way. We've also included the best times to visit each destination, helping you choose the perfect moment to capture the essence of each place. Whether it's the lush greenery of spring or the golden hues of fall, Oregon's seasonal panoramas are not to be missed.

Understanding the practicalities of travel, each destination entry outlines any tolls or access fees, ensuring you're prepared before you arrive. Fascinating trivia for each location offers insights and stories that enhance the depth of your visit, while up-to-date website links keep you informed on the latest at each destination.

As an exclusive bonus, this guide comes with an interactive state map pre-loaded with all 120 destinations. This digital companion is designed to streamline your planning and navigation, eliminating the usual hassle of map-reading and ensuring you make the most of your time exploring Oregon.

Oregon Bucket List is your gateway to adventure, a comprehensive guide that promises not just to guide your way, but to inspire and exhilarate. Whether you're tracing the footsteps of pioneers, gazing at the wonders of nature, or soaking in the cultural landscapes, your Oregon adventure starts here. So lace up your boots, grab your guide, and prepare to embark on a journey where each destination is a dream realized and every moment is a memory in the making. Are you ready to discover, explore, and create your own Oregon story? Let's set off!

ABOUT OREGON

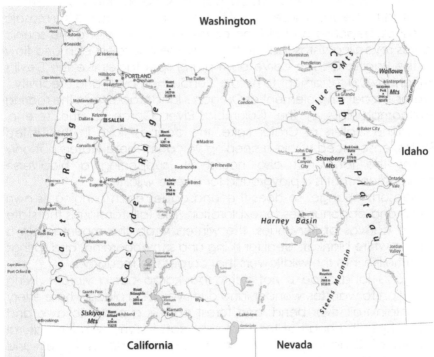

To access the <u>Digital Map</u>, please refer to the 'Map Chapter' in this book

Landscape of Oregon

Oregon's landscape is a breathtaking canvas of nature's artistry, a place where the wild and the serene harmoniously intertwine, inviting the explorer to immerse themselves in its vast and varied beauty. This Pacific Northwest state is a treasure trove of geographical wonders, sculpted by volcanic activity and shaped by the relentless forces of wind and water over millennia.

The majestic Cascades stretch across the state, crowned by the iconic Mount Hood, whose snow-capped peak is a beacon for adventurers and nature lovers alike. These mountains are not merely peaks but are gatekeepers to lush, expansive forests rich with Douglas firs and red cedars that whisper tales of the ancient earth beneath their roots. The shadows of these towering giants stretch across the High Desert, where the land tells a different story, one of sagebrush plains and juniper hills that glow amber at sunset.

To the west, the Oregon Coast, with its rugged cliffs and whimsical rock formations like the famed Haystack Rock, offers a dramatic contrast to the tranquil beauty of the inland. The coastline is a mosaic of sandy beaches and hidden coves, each turn along the scenic routes revealing vistas that stir the soul. The ceaseless ebb and flow of the Pacific Ocean carve out natural spectacles like the Devil's Punchbowl, a testament to nature's enduring power and creativity.

Water is a defining element of Oregon's landscape, from the roaring Multnomah Falls in the Columbia River Gorge to the serene, crystalline waters of Crater Lake, the deepest lake in the United States, ensconced within a sleeping volcano. These waters not only sculpt the land but also nourish it, supporting a biodiverse environment that is a playground for diverse wildlife.

As seasons change, so does the landscape, each bringing its own flavor and opportunities for exploration. The fall transforms the state into a canvas of fiery hues, the winters wrap the mountains in a pristine white blanket, ideal for skiing and snowboarding, and springs breathe life into the wildflowers that carpet the meadows.

Oregon's landscape is not just a backdrop but a vibrant, living invitation to wander, wonder, and discover. It's a place where every mountain trail, river bend, and forest path is a portal to awe and adventure. The heart of the explorer beats in sync with the natural rhythm of Oregon, each visit promising new stories to tell and memories to cherish.

Flora and Fauna of Oregon

The flora and fauna of Oregon paint a vivid tableau of biodiversity and natural splendor, showcasing an ecological richness that few places on Earth can match. Oregon's botanical landscape is a lush, verdant tapestry woven from both common and rare plant species that thrive across varied habitats—from the coastal headlands to the rugged high desert.

In the misty realms of the coastal forests, ancient Sitka spruces tower skyward, their massive limbs cloaked in dense mosses and dripping with ferns. These primeval woodlands are home to the iconic Douglas fir, a symbol of the Pacific Northwest, standing sentinel over the understory filled with vibrant rhododendrons and delicate trilliums. As one ventures inland, the scenery shifts to the rolling hills and sunlit valleys of the Willamette Valley, where wildflowers such as the Oregon iris and camas splash color across the meadows, and the air is perfumed with the sweet scent of wild lilac.

Oregon's fauna is as diverse as its landscapes. The dense forests provide sanctuary to an array of wildlife, including elusive cougars, majestic elk, and the stately Roosevelt elk. The high desert echoes with the calls of pronghorns, while its sagebrush seas offer refuge to the greater sage-grouse, an icon of the American West. Along the rocky coastal shores, colonies of sea lions bask in the sun, and tufted puffins nest on cliffside burrows, their bright beaks adding splashes of color to the grey stone.

Bird enthusiasts will find Oregon a paradise, with opportunities to observe a spectacular variety of species, from the majestic bald eagles soaring above the Columbia River Gorge to the colorful western tanagers flitting through the canopy. The rivers and lakes are teeming with life, supporting vibrant communities of salmon and trout, which in turn draw hungry ospreys and patient herons to their waters.

Exploring Oregon's flora and fauna is to embark on a journey through a living museum of natural history, each species and habitat telling a story of adaptation and survival. It's a realm where nature's beauty is displayed in its most raw and enchanting forms, inviting all who visit to share in its timeless wonder.

Climate of Oregon

Oregon's climate is as diverse and enchanting as its landscapes, offering a symphony of weather patterns that create a state of perpetual beauty and intrigue. From the mist-kissed shores of the Pacific Coast to the sun-drenched expanses of the High Desert, Oregon's climate shapes the experiences of all who wander its varied terrains.

The coast, with its cool, maritime influence, is a realm where soft fogs curl around towering sea stacks and gentle rains nourish verdant forests. Here, the air is crisp and invigorating, perfect for reflective walks along endless beaches or cozy afternoons in coastal cafes. The sound of the ocean is a constant backdrop, its rhythm syncing with the steady beat of light coastal showers that bring the landscape to life.

Transitioning inland, the Willamette Valley offers a milder, more temperate version of the Pacific Northwest climate. This fertile crescent, cradled between cascading mountain ranges, is blessed with a generous mix of sunny days and refreshing rainfalls, creating ideal conditions for the lush vineyards and bountiful orchards that dot the landscape. Spring in the valley is a spectacle of blooming flowers and buzzing bees, while autumn cloaks the hills in spectacular shades of gold and crimson.

As one ascends into the Cascade Range, the air grows crisp and the snow begins to fall, transforming the region into a winter wonderland. The high elevations receive copious amounts of snow, perfect for skiing, snowboarding, and other winter sports. The sharp contrast of deep blue skies against the stark white snowpack is breathtaking, offering a pristine escape into nature's solitude.

Further east, the climate dries dramatically in the expansive Oregon High Desert. Here, sunny days dominate the year, casting long shadows over the sagebrush and juniper landscapes. Nights are cool, and the clear skies provide an astronomer's paradise, with star-filled nights that inspire dreams of distant galaxies.

Each season in Oregon brings its own charm, from the delicate cherry blossoms of spring to the fiery leaves of fall, from the summer's sunlit days to the quiet of winter's snow. This climatic diversity not only defines the character of the region but also invites visitors to experience a year-round adventure that is as varied as it is enchanting. In Oregon, the weather is not just a condition but an integral part of the state's mesmerizing allure.

History of Oregon

Oregon's history is a captivating narrative of transformation and resilience, spanning centuries of indigenous heritage, pioneering spirits, and innovative developments that together weave the rich tapestry that defines the state today. From its earliest inhabitants to the complex multicultural society it hosts now, Oregon exemplifies a unique convergence of histories, each contributing to its vibrant culture and dynamic identity.

Before European explorers set foot in the Pacific Northwest, diverse tribes and indigenous peoples thrived across what is now Oregon. These communities, including the Chinook, the Klamath, and the Umpqua, among others, developed rich traditions, sophisticated societal structures, and sustainable practices that perfectly adapted to the bountiful yet varied landscapes of the region. These first

Oregonians lived in harmony with the land, cultivating a deep understanding of its flora, fauna, and seasonal rhythms that later newcomers would rely on.

The arrival of European explorers in the 18th century marked the beginning of a new era. It was an age driven by the quest for new trade routes and territorial expansion, with the Oregon Coast witnessing the first European feet with the landing of Spanish, British, and later American explorers. Notably, the Lewis and Clark expedition of the early 1800s, sent by President Thomas Jefferson, marked a significant turning point, opening the floodgates for waves of settlers who would traverse the treacherous trails in pursuit of new lives in the fertile lands of the Oregon territory.

The mid-19th century was defined by the Oregon Trail, a 2,170-mile wagon route that beckoned over 400,000 settlers westward, drawn by the promise of land and opportunity. This mass migration was not without conflict and tragedy, often resulting in displacement and hardship for the native populations. The history of Oregon is deeply intertwined with this trail, reflecting a period of rapid growth, significant upheaval, and profound transformation of the land.

As Oregon transitioned into statehood in 1859, it became a battleground for various social and political ideologies, particularly around issues of slavery and native rights. The state's early economy was dominated by the timber industry, exploiting the vast forests that defined its landscape. As the 20th century unfolded, Oregon emerged as a hub of innovation and environmental awareness. The establishment of public lands, the environmental movement spearheaded by Governor Tom McCall, and the bold urban planning initiatives like the Oregon Beach Bill, which granted public access to the state's beaches, exemplified a progressive attitude towards natural conservation and community welfare.

Today, Oregon's history continues to evolve, with its past ever-present in the protected historical sites, museums, and cultural practices that celebrate the state's diverse heritage. The blend of ancient traditions with the pioneering spirit and progressive innovations offers a unique lens through which to view and experience Oregon. From the Native American festivals that celebrate centuries-old traditions to the modern cultural festivals in Portland and beyond, Oregon's history is alive, celebrated, and deeply respected.

This history not only offers a window into the past but also enriches every visit to the state's stunning landscapes and vibrant communities. Whether exploring the ancient forests, walking the paths of early pioneers, or enjoying the contemporary cities that reflect a commitment to sustainability and diversity, visitors to Oregon walk through layers of history that speak of endurance, change, and hope. Each corner of the state, from the rugged coastlines and majestic mountains to the serene high deserts and lush valleys, tells a story of a past replete with challenges and triumphs—a story that invites everyone to explore, learn, and be inspired.

How to Use this Guide

Welcome to your comprehensive guide to exploring Oregon! This chapter is dedicated to helping you understand how to effectively use this guide and the interactive map to enhance your travel experience. Let's dive into the simple steps to navigate the book and utilize the digital tools provided, ensuring you have the best adventure possible.

Understanding the Guide's Structure

The guide features 120 of the best destinations across the beautiful state of Oregon, thoughtfully compiled to inspire and facilitate your explorations. These destinations are divided into areas and listed alphabetically. This organization aims to simplify your search process, making it quick and intuitive to locate each destination in the book.

Using the Alphabetical Listings

Since the destination areas are arranged alphabetically, you can easily flip through the guide to find a specific place or browse areas that catch your interest. Each destination entry in the book includes essential information such as:

- A vivid description of the destination.

- The complete address and the nearest major city, giving you a quick geographical context.

- GPS coordinates for precise navigation.

- The best times to visit, helping you plan your trip according to seasonal attractions and weather.

- Details on tolls or access fees, preparing you for any costs associated with your visit.

- Fun trivia to enhance your knowledge and appreciation of each location.

- A link to the official website for up-to-date information.

To further enhance your experience and save time, you can scan these website links using apps like <u>Google Lens</u> to open them directly without the need to type them into a browser. This seamless integration allows for quicker access to the latest information and resources about each destination.

Navigating with the Interactive State Map

Your guide comes equipped with an innovative tool—an interactive map of Oregon that integrates seamlessly with Google Maps. This digital map is pre-loaded with all 120 destinations, offering an effortless way to visualize and plan your journey across the state.

How to Use the Map:

- Open the Interactive Map: Start by accessing the digital map through the link provided in your guide. You can open it on any device that supports Google Maps, such as a smartphone, tablet, or computer.

- Choose Your Starting Point: Decide where you will begin your adventure. You might start from your current location or another specific point in Oregon.

- Explore Nearby Destinations: With the map open, zoom in and out to view the destinations near your starting point. Click on any marker to see a brief description and access quick links for navigation and more details.

- Plan Your Itinerary: Based on the destinations close to your chosen start, you can create a personalized itinerary. You can select multiple locations to visit in a day or plan a more extended road trip through various regions.

Combining the Book and Map for Best Results

To get the most out of your adventures:

- Cross-Reference: Use the interactive map to spot destinations you are interested in and then refer back to the guidebook for detailed information and insights.

- Plan Sequentially: As you plan your route on the map, use the alphabetical listing in the book to easily gather information on each destination and organize your visits efficiently.

- Stay Updated: Regularly check the provided website links for any changes in operation hours, fees, or special events at the destinations.

By following these guidelines and utilizing both the guidebook and the interactive map, you will be well-equipped to explore Oregon's diverse landscapes and attractions. Whether you are seeking solitude in nature, adventure in the outdoors, or cultural experiences in urban settings, this guide will serve as your reliable companion, ensuring every adventure is memorable and every discovery is enriching. Happy travels!

ARCH CAPE

Hug Point State Park

Escape to the rugged beauty of Hug Point State Park, where ocean meets an enchanting forested coastline just a few miles south of Cannon Beach. Explore its sandy coves, seasonal waterfalls, and intriguing caves once used by stagecoaches, evident from the visible wheel ruts in the rock. Located off the scenic Highway 101, this park offers visitors a perfect mix of history and natural splendor with opportunities to picnic, hike the short trails, or explore tide pools teeming with life during low tide.

Location: Hug Point State Recreation Site, Beach Access Rd, Arch Cape, OR 97102, USA

Closest City or Town: Arch Cape, Oregon

How to Get There: From Cannon Beach, head south on US-101 S for about 5 miles. Follow the signs to Hug Point State Park, turning right onto Beach Access Rd.

GPS Coordinates: 45.8316734° N, 123.9615812° W

Best Time to Visit: Summer for the best weather and low tides revealing more of the beach and tide pools.

Pass/Permit/Fees: Access to the park is free.

Did You Know? Hug Point got its name from the need to '"hug'" the point closely with stagecoaches traveling along the beach at low tide!

Website:
https://stateparks.oregon.gov/index.cfm?do=park.profile&parkId=137

Oswald West State Park

Discover the enchanting Oswald West State Park, a haven nestled amidst the dramatic landscape of Oregon's coastline. This park offers a lush, temperate rainforest that opens to the spectacular vistas of the Pacific Ocean. Ideal for an adventurous day out, you can surf at

Short Sand Beach, hike along the secluded trails or simply relish the solitude on a scenic overlook. Just off Highway 101, it embodies the spirit of the Oregon Coast with its astonishing biodiversity and continuous opportunities for discovery and solitude.

Location: Oswald West State Park, Arch Cape, OR 97102, USA

Closest City or Town: Arch Cape, Oregon

How to Get There: Travel along US-101 N; the park is located between Cannon Beach and Manzanita. Look for the signage and turn west into the park.

GPS Coordinates: 45.7698110° N, 123.9590931° W

Best Time to Visit: Spring through fall, for ideal hiking and surfing conditions.

Pass/Permit/Fees: No entrance fees required.

Did You Know? This park is named after Oswald West, the 14th Governor of Oregon, who worked to establish policies preserving Oregon's beaches for public use.

Website: https://stateparks.oregon.gov/index.cfm?do=park.profile&parkId=139

ASHLAND

Lithia Park

Step into Ashland's crown jewel, Lithia Park, where carefully tended gardens, rippling streams, and ancient forests come together in a perfect symphony of nature. Located in the heart of Ashland, this park stretches over 93 acres from the bustling downtown to the quiet, reflective outskirts. Engage in a myriad of activities from duck feeding, playing tennis, to watching a live performance at the bandshell. Lithia Park is not just a park; it's a vibrant community hub reflecting Ashland's cultural and natural heritage.

Location: 59 Winburn Way, Ashland, OR 97520-2735

Closest City or Town: Ashland, Oregon

How to Get There: Located downtown, it is easily reachable by foot from anywhere in central Ashland, or by car from I-5, taking exit 14 to Ashland.

GPS Coordinates: 42.1882321° N, 122.7166648° W

Best Time to Visit: Spring and fall for mild weather and beautiful foliage.

Pass/Permit/Fees: No entrance fees.

Did You Know? The park's name originates from the lithium-rich waters found in the park's natural springs.

Website: http://www.nps.gov/nr/travel/ashland/lit.htm

Oregon Shakespeare Festival

Immerse yourself in the theatrical arts at the Oregon Shakespeare Festival in Ashland, renowned for its dynamic performances attracting theater lovers worldwide. Situated in Ashland's quaint downtown, the festival runs from February to November, offering a full roster of classic and modern plays. Beyond the stage, engage with actors in discussions, pursuing a deeper understanding of the productions. Imaginatively staged, each performance at the festival promises a unique blend of intellectual stimulation and unbridled entertainment.

Location: 15 S Pioneer St, Ashland, OR 97520-2749

Closest City or Town: Ashland, Oregon

How to Get There: In central Ashland, it is accessible via I-5, taking the exit for OR-99 to downtown Ashland.

GPS Coordinates: 42.1961589° N, 122.7146233° W

Best Time to Visit: During the festival seasons—spring, summer, and fall.

Pass/Permit/Fees: Tickets required for performances; prices vary.

Did You Know? This is one of the oldest and largest professional nonprofit theatres in the United States.

Website: http://www.osfashland.org/

ASTORIA

Astoria Column

Unveil panoramic views of the Columbia River, the Pacific Ocean, and the encompassing landscapes atop the Astoria Column. Towering 125 feet, this artistic pinnacle is adorned with a spiraling frieze that chronicles the significant events of the region's history. Positioned on Coxcomb Hill, it not only serves as a historical marker but also as a breathtaking viewpoint, drawing visitors to ascend its 164-step spiral staircase for an unmatched aerial glimpse of Astoria's natural splendor.

Location: 1 Coxcomb Drive, Astoria, OR 97103

Closest City or Town: Astoria, Oregon

How to Get There: From downtown Astoria, take 15th street uphill until it becomes Coxcomb Drive. Follow up the hill to the column.

GPS Coordinates: 46.1813205° N, 123.8175132° W

Best Time to Visit: Year-round, but the views are clearest from spring through fall.

Pass/Permit/Fees: A small parking fee applies.

Did You Know? The Column was completed in 1926 and is part of a series of historical markers erected across the U.S. by the Great Northern Railway.

Website: http://astoriacolumn.org/

Columbia River Maritime Museum

Uncover the secrets of the mighty Columbia River at the Columbia River Maritime Museum, a treasure trove of maritime lore located in the charming coastal town of Astoria, Oregon. Step inside to discover an array of engaging exhibits that chronicle the perilous waters of the Columbia River Bar, famed as the 'Graveyard of the Pacific'. From historic shipwrecks to the science of oceanography, each display offers a deep dive into the maritime heritage of the Northwest.

Location: 1792 Marine Dr, Astoria, OR 97103-3525

Closest City or Town: Astoria, Oregon

How to Get There: Located in downtown Astoria, easily accessible by following the US-101 N to Marine Drive.

GPS Coordinates: 46.1898801° N, 123.8236049° W

Best Time to Visit: Spring through fall for milder weather and comprehensive touring.

Pass/Permit/Fees: Admission is charged; visit the website for current rates.

Did You Know? The museum is home to one of the few floating lighthouse ships in the world, the Lightship Columbia.

Website: http://www.crmm.org/

Astoria-Megler Bridge

Find yourself above the clouds as you cross the Astoria-Megler Bridge, a marvel of engineering stretching across the lower Columbia River. Linking Oregon to Washington, this bridge offers panoramic views that are particularly mesmerizing at sunset. Not just a functional route, it stands as a symbol of unity and achievement, dominating the skyline with its impressive length and graceful architecture.

Location: Oregon Coast Hwy, Astoria, OR 97103

Closest City or Town: Astoria, Oregon

How to Get There: The bridge is easily accessible via US Highway 101, connecting Astoria, Oregon to Point Ellice, Washington.

GPS Coordinates: 46.1903149° N, 123.8493544° W

Best Time to Visit: Summer for the best visibility and weather conditions.

Pass/Permit/Fees: No toll or fee for crossing.

Did You Know? At its completion in 1966, it was the longest continuous truss bridge in the world.

Website: http://oregoncoastbridges.com/excerpt1.html

Fort Clatsop National Memorial

Journey back to the winter of 1805-06 at Fort Clatsop National Memorial, where the Lewis and Clark Expedition hunkered down after their historic trek across the American continent. Experience life as it was through reconstructed log structures, interpretive trails, and live historical demonstrations, all set within the dense, verdant forests of Oregon's coastal landscape.

Location: 92343 Fort Clatsop Rd, Astoria, OR 97103-8701

Closest City or Town: Astoria, Oregon

How to Get There: Take US-101 S from Astoria to Fort Clatsop Road, then follow the signs to the memorial.

GPS Coordinates: 46.1366944° N, 123.8783871° W

Best Time to Visit: Summer and early fall for reenactments and pleasant weather.

Pass/Permit/Fees: Entrance fee required; check the website for details.

Did You Know? The fort's name, Clatsop, stems from the local Native American tribe that helped the explorers survive the winter.

Website: http://www.nps.gov/lewi/planyourvisit/fortclatsop.htm

Astoria Riverfront Trolley

Embark on a scenic jaunt along the Astoria waterfront aboard the historic Astoria Riverfront Trolley. Known affectionately as '"Old 300,"' this charming trolley car offers a narrated ride that highlights the rich tapestry of Astoria's past and present, from bustling canneries to tranquil marinas, all lining the majestic Columbia River.

Location: 480 Industry St, Astoria, OR 97103, USA

Closest City or Town: Astoria, Oregon

How to Get There: The trolley runs along the riverfront; start at the east end of Astoria near the Maritime Museum.

GPS Coordinates: 46.1857854° N, 123.8590128° W

Best Time to Visit: Spring through fall when the trolley is most frequently in operation.

Pass/Permit/Fees: Small fare required; see the website for details.

Did You Know? The trolley itself is over 100 years old, originally serving in San Antonio, Texas before coming to Astoria.

Website: https://www.travelastoria.com/trip-ideas/ride-the-historic-trolley.html

Flavel House Museum

Explore the gilded age elegance of the Flavel House Museum in Astoria, where Victorian architecture meets the intriguing history of a family that shaped the region. Wander through this beautifully preserved mansion, with its intricate woodwork and period furnishings, and step into a time of prosperity and challenge on the Oregon coast.

Location: 441 8th St, Astoria, OR 97103-4620

Closest City or Town: Astoria, Oregon

How to Get There: In downtown Astoria, accessible from US-30 or US-101, follow signs to the city center.

GPS Coordinates: 46.1878730° N, 123.8355395° W

Best Time to Visit: Year-round, with special events during holidays.

Pass/Permit/Fees: A modest entry fee is charged; details available on the website.

Did You Know? Captain George Flavel was one of Astoria's first millionaires and a noted bar pilot on the Columbia River.

Website: http://astoriamuseums.org/"

Astoria Oregon Riverwalk

Discover the charm of Astoria as you stroll along the Astoria Oregon Riverwalk, a gateway to the rich maritime and cultural heritage of this historic port city. With the Columbia River to guide your path, the Riverwalk offers enchanting views combined with easy access to museums, galleries, and quaint eateries that lie along its course. This picturesque pathway is lined with relics of Astoria's vibrant past, from the restored trolley tracks to the echoes of sea lions. A walk here not only connects you with nature but envelopes you in stories centuries old.

Location: Riverwalk Trail, Astoria Riverwalk, Astoria, OR 97103, USA

Closest City or Town: Astoria, Oregon

How to Get There: Access the Riverwalk by starting from downtown Astoria. Public parking is available along Marine Drive or at the Maritime Museum, which is centrally located to the Riverwalk.

GPS Coordinates: 46.1981099° N, 123.7755306° W

Best Time to Visit: Spring through fall, when the weather is mild and the views are picturesque.

Pass/Permit/Fees: Free to access.

Did You Know? The Astoria Riverwalk is home to the Old 300 trolley, a restored historic streetcar that offers rides and guided tours along the waterfront.

Website: https://en.wikipedia.org/wiki/Astoria,_Oregon

The Lewis And Clark National And State Historical Parks

Step back in time at The Lewis And Clark National And State Historical Parks, where the epic journey of America's pioneering explorers, Lewis and Clark, is commemorated. Nestled in the lush landscapes of Oregon, these parks span several sites, offering a thrilling glimpse into the challenges and triumphs faced by the expedition. Hiking, viewing historical reenactments, and exploring interactive exhibits make for an immersive historical experience. This destination is not just a park, but a proud reminder of America's adventurous spirit.

Location: 92343 Fort Clatsop Rd, Astoria, OR 97103-8701

Closest City or Town: Astoria, Oregon

How to Get There: From Astoria, take US-101 S to Oregon Hwy 104, follow signs for Lewis and Clark National Historical Park.

GPS Coordinates: 46.1344995° N, 123.8803086° W

Best Time to Visit: Summer and early fall for the best weather and full schedule of events.

Pass/Permit/Fees: Entry fee required; details on the park website.

Did You Know? The park features a replica of the Fort Clatsop, the winter encampment of the Lewis and Clark Expedition.

Website: http://www.nps.gov/lewi

BAKER CITY

National Historic Oregon Trail Interpretive Center

Journey through the pivotal paths of pioneers at the National Historic Oregon Trail Interpretive Center. Located near Baker City, this comprehensive center offers vivid reenactments, interactive exhibits, and miles of preserved trails. Visitors are transported to the 19th century as they walk in the footsteps of thousands who ventured West seeking new beginnings. The real-life stories and scenic landscapes provide a profound connection to America's frontier history.

Location: 22267 Oregon Highway 86, Baker City, OR 97814-6016

Closest City or Town: Baker City, Oregon

How to Get There: From Baker City, head east on Hwy 86 for about 5 miles. The center is well-signposted from the highway.

GPS Coordinates: 44.8148244° N, 117.7286307° W

Best Time to Visit: Late spring through early fall; especially engaging during live reenactment events.

Pass/Permit/Fees: Admission fee applies; check the website for current rates.

Did You Know? The site overlooks the famous Flagstaff Hill, a vantage point where emigrants first viewed the Oregon Trail.

Website: https://www.blm.gov/learn/interpretive-centers/national-historic-oregon-trail-interpretive-center

BANDON

Face Rock State Scenic Viewpoint

Unveil the legend of Face Rock at Face Rock State Scenic Viewpoint in Bandon, Oregon. Myth intertwines with stunning natural beauty here, where the face-shaped rock gazes eternally skyward from the ocean. Local lore tells of an Indian maiden frozen by an evil spirit. Beyond folklore, the site offers breathtaking sunsets and a chance to spot whales. It's a photographer's delight and a serene spot for contemplation or beach strolls under the watch of Face Rock.

Location: Off US 101, Bandon, OR 97411

Closest City or Town: Bandon, Oregon

How to Get There: Take US-101 to Bandon. Turn west onto Fillmore Avenue which leads directly to the viewpoint.

GPS Coordinates: 43.1063175° N, 124.4353381° W

Best Time to Visit: Year-round, though sunsets are particularly spectacular during the summer.

Pass/Permit/Fees: Free access.

Did You Know? According to Native American legend, you can hear a maiden's voice at night when the wind is right.

Website: http://www.oregonstateparks.org/park_66.php

Coquille River Lighthouse

Navigate your way to the Coquille River Lighthouse, where maritime history illuminates the Oregon coast. Established in 1896, this historic beacon guided mariners past the treacherous sandbars of Bandon. Today, visitors can tour the lighthouse, learn about its storied past, and enjoy panoramic views of the Coquille River and Pacific Ocean. The surrounding environment offers rich wildlife viewing, particularly of migratory birds and occasional sea lions.

Location: 56487 Bullards Beach Rd, Bandon, OR 97411, USA

Closest City or Town: Bandon, Oregon

How to Get There: From Bandon, follow Highway 101 north. Turn west onto Bullards Beach State Park and follow the signs to the lighthouse.

GPS Coordinates: 43.1238937° N, 124.4242522° W

Best Time to Visit: May through September, when tours are typically available.

Pass/Permit/Fees: No fee for accessing the lighthouse; state park parking fee may apply.

Did You Know? The lighthouse was deactivated in 1939 and is now listed on the National Register of Historic Places.

Website:
https://www.fs.usda.gov/recarea/crgnsa/recarea/?recid=29934"

BEND

High Desert Museum

Uncover the vibrant spirit of the Oregon outback at the High Desert Museum, a captivating establishment just south of Bend. Here, visitors are treated to close encounters with native wildlife and insights into the rich history of the Pacific Northwest. Engaging exhibits range from living history performances to immersive dioramas, offering something of interest for every age. Nestled amidst the scenic byways of Highway 97, it's an educational sanctuary where the high desert comes to life through art, science, history, and culture.

Location: 59800 S Highway 97, Bend, OR 97702-7963

Closest City or Town: Bend, Oregon

How to Get There: From Bend, head south on US-97 for about 5 miles. The museum entrance is signposted on your right.

GPS Coordinates: 43.9661759° N, 121.3419191° W

Best Time to Visit: Year-round, with special events and exhibits frequently updated.

Pass/Permit/Fees: Entry fee required, check the website for current prices.

Did You Know? The museum showcases a stunning, real-time working exhibit called the "'Autumn's Wildlife Rehabilitation Center,'" where you can observe staff caring for injured wildlife.

Website: http://www.highdesertmuseum.org/

Newberry National Volcanic Monument

Venture into the heart of Central Oregon's volcanic landscape at the Newberry National Volcanic Monument. Located east of Bend in the Deschutes National Forest, this geological wonder invites adventurers to explore its massive caldera, lava flows, and stunning obsidian flows. Hiking, fishing, and caving are popular activities here, offering a firsthand experience of the region's volcanic origins. The monument's highlight, the Newberry Caldera, encircles the twin lakes of Paulina and East, providing a picturesque setting for a day of exploration.

Location: 1645 Hwy. 20 E Deschutes National Forest, Bend, OR 97701

Closest City or Town: Bend, Oregon

How to Get There: Drive about 20 minutes east from Bend on Highway 20. Follow signs directing you to the monument.

GPS Coordinates: 44.0915566° N, 121.2610823° W

Best Time to Visit: Summer and early fall for the most accessible trails and viewpoints.

Pass/Permit/Fees: Day-use fee required; annual passes are also accepted.

Did You Know? The monument includes Lava River Cave, Oregon's longest known lava tube, which you can explore with a rented lantern.

Website: http://www.fs.fed.us/r6/centraloregon/newberrynvm/index.shtml

Pilot Butte State Scenic Viewpoint

Elevate your view at Pilot Butte State Scenic Viewpoint, a unique landmark in the heart of Bend, Oregon. This ancient volcano offers a panoramic vista of the high desert and the snow-capped Cascade Range after a rewarding ascent, either by foot or by car. It's a popular spot for both dawn and sunset watchers, providing a 360-degree overview that includes Mount Hood, Mount Jefferson, and the Three Sisters.

Location: US 20, Bend, OR 97701

Closest City or Town: Bend, Oregon

How to Get There: Pilot Butte is easily accessible from US 20. There's parking available at the base for those who prefer to hike up.

GPS Coordinates: 44.0948422° N, 121.3028149° W

Best Time to Visit: Accessible year-round, but sunrise or sunset times are particularly spectacular.

Pass/Permit/Fees: No entrance fees.

Did You Know? Pilot Butte is one of just four extinct volcanoes located within a U.S. city's limits.

Website: http://www.oregonstateparks.org/park_42.php

Tumalo Falls

Discover the jewel of Central Oregon, Tumalo Falls. Just a short drive from Bend, this stunning 97-foot waterfall offers breathtaking views and a variety of hiking trails that range from easy to moderate in difficulty. The drive itself to Tumalo Falls, passing through thick forests and alongside rushing streams, is as picturesque as the destination. Once there, follow the trails for different perspectives, or enjoy a picnic overlooking the falls.

Location: Oregon 97703, USA

Closest City or Town: Bend, Oregon

How to Get There: Take Skyliners Road out of Bend and follow the signs for Tumalo Falls. The last few miles are on a well-maintained gravel road.

GPS Coordinates: 44.0339557° N, 121.5668789° W

Best Time to Visit: Spring and early summer when the water flow is at its peak.

Pass/Permit/Fees: Parking fee required; Northwest Forest Pass may be used.

Did You Know? In winter, the falls transform into a frozen cascade, offering dramatic icy scenes popular with photographers.

Website:
https://stateparks.oregon.gov/index.cfm?do=park.profile&parkId=34

Mt. Bachelor Ski Area

Hit the slopes at Mt. Bachelor, a premier destination for winter sports enthusiasts in the Pacific Northwest. Located just west of Bend, Oregon, this ski area offers a variety of runs to suit all skill levels, from gentle groomed trails to challenging black diamonds. The area is renowned for its light, dry snow, extensive backcountry access, and long skiing seasons. In summer, Mt. Bachelor transforms into a playground for mountain biking, hiking, and scenic chairlift rides.

Location: 13000 SW Century Dr, Bend, OR 97702-3595

Closest City or Town: Bend, Oregon

How to Get There: Drive west from Bend on Century Drive towards Mt. Bachelor.

GPS Coordinates: 43.9844004° N, 121.4951847° W

Best Time to Visit: Winter for skiing and summer for outdoor activities.

Pass/Permit/Fees: Lift tickets required for skiing; prices vary. Summer activities may have different rates.

Did You Know? Mt. Bachelor is one of the largest ski resorts in the United States by acreage.

Website: http://www.mtbachelor.com/"

Lava River Cave

Discover the underworld wonders at Lava River Cave, a natural lava tube where adventure meets history. Located in the high desert near Bend, Oregon, this cave offers a thrilling walk through Oregon's volcanic past. Equipped with a flashlight, you can navigate the mile-long tube, exploring the rocky terrain and eerie silence that lies beneath the surface. This hidden gem provides a cool escape from the summer heat and a fascinating glimpse into geological formations.

Location: Cottonwood Rd, Bend, OR 97707, USA

Closest City or Town: Bend, Oregon

How to Get There: From Bend, travel south on US-97 S for about 12 miles, then take exit 151 for Cottonwood Road. Follow the signs to Lava River Cave.

GPS Coordinates: 43.8954° N, 121.3696° W

Best Time to Visit: Late spring through early fall when the cave is accessible.

Pass/Permit/Fees: A small fee is charged for entry; visit the website for current rates.

Did You Know? Lava River Cave is the longest continuous lava tube in Oregon, making it an intriguing study for both geologists and adventurers alike.

Website:
https://www.fs.usda.gov/recarea/deschutes/recarea/?recid=38396

Lava Lands Visitor Center

Embark on an educational journey at Lava Lands Visitor Center, where the tumultuous volcanic history of the Northwest comes to life. Located just south of Bend, the center sits amidst the rugged beauty of Oregon's volcanic landscape. Visitors can enjoy interactive exhibits, scenic trails, and panoramic views from the observatory. This gateway to the Newberry National Volcanic Monument offers unique insights into the region's geology and natural history, making it a must-visit for nature lovers and families.

Location: 58201 South Highway 97, Bend, OR 97702

Closest City or Town: Bend, Oregon

How to Get There: Directly accessible via US-97 S, the visitor center is clearly marked with signage along the highway.

GPS Coordinates: 43.9099° N, 121.3569° W

Best Time to Visit: Summer and early fall for the best access to trails and exhibits.

Pass/Permit/Fees: Entry fees apply; check the website for details.

Did You Know? The observatory at Lava Lands offers one of the best views of the Cascade Mountains' volcanic range.

Website:
https://www.fs.usda.gov/recarea/deschutes/recarea/?recid=38394

BRIDAL VEIL

Multnomah Falls

Step into the enchanting world of Multnomah Falls, Oregon's tallest waterfall, beckoning visitors with its majestic beauty. Located in the heart of the Columbia River Gorge, this 620-foot waterfall offers a mesmerizing sight with easy accessibility. The historic Benson Bridge allows an up-close view and perfect photo opportunities. Beyond the falls, hiking trails wind through lush forests, offering more adventures and stunning vistas. It's a place where the roar of the falls and the serene nature surroundings create an unforgettable experience.

Location: 53000 E Historic Columbia River Hwy, Bridal Veil, OR 97010

Closest City or Town: Bridal Veil, Oregon

How to Get There: Accessible via I-84 E, take exit 31 for a direct route to the parking area and falls.

GPS Coordinates: 45.6033° N, 122.0424° W

Best Time to Visit: Spring and fall for optimal water flow and fewer crowds.

Pass/Permit/Fees: No entrance fee, but parking fees may apply.

Did You Know? Multnomah Falls is the second highest year-round waterfall in the United States.

Website:
http://www.fs.usda.gov/recarea/crgnsa/recarea/?recid=30026

BROOKINGS

Harris Beach State Park

Lose yourself in the stunning beauty of Harris Beach State Park, where the rugged Oregon coast meets rich biodiversity. This park, located in Brookings, features sandy beaches dotted with rocky outcrops and tide pools. It's an ideal spot for beachcombing, photography, and wildlife viewing, especially during the migration seasons of gray whales and myriad bird species. Campsites with ocean views add to the appeal, making it a perfect coastal retreat.

Location: U.S. 101, Brookings, OR 97415, USA

Closest City or Town: Brookings, Oregon

How to Get There: Situated along U.S. 101, it is easily accessible by car with ample signage.

GPS Coordinates: 42.0659° N, 124.3046° W

Best Time to Visit: Summer for the best weather and winter for whale watching.

Pass/Permit/Fees: Day-use is free; camping fees apply.

Did You Know? Harris Beach State Park is named after George Harris, a Scottish pioneer who settled here in the late 19th century.

Website:
https://stateparks.oregon.gov/index.cfm?do=park.profile&parkId=5
8

CANNON BEACH

Haystack Rock

Experience the iconic Haystack Rock, a towering sea stack that dominates Cannon Beach's scenic landscape. This 235-foot rock is not just a photographer's paradise but also a protected marine garden. Visitors can explore the surrounding tide pools, home to colorful starfish, crabs, and sea anemones. During low tide, the base of the rock becomes accessible, offering a closer look at its vibrant marine ecosystem. Additionally, it's a critical nesting site for puffins and other seabirds, making it an important location for bird watchers.

Location: Us 101, Cannon Beach, OR 97110

Closest City or Town: Cannon Beach, Oregon

How to Get There: Haystack Rock is best reached by following US-101 to Cannon Beach, with direct access to the beach areas.

GPS Coordinates: 45.8841° N, 123.9685° W

Best Time to Visit: Late spring through early fall for the best tide pooling and bird watching.

Pass/Permit/Fees: No fees are required to visit, but parking in Cannon Beach may be regulated.

Did You Know? Haystack Rock is one of the most photographed landmarks on the Oregon coast, featured in numerous films and TV shows.

Website: https://it.wikipedia.org/wiki/Haystack_Rock

Cannon Beach

Delight in the quintessential Oregon coast experience at Cannon Beach, a picturesque seaside town that is home to the iconic Haystack Rock. Imagine standing on the soft sands, the waves gently kissing your feet, with the massive, monolithic rock formation standing sentinel in the background. Located in the charming town of Cannon Beach, this destination offers breathtaking views and a serene atmosphere perfect for beachcombing, photography, and simply soaking in the sunsets that paint the sky vibrant colors each evening.

Location: 124 N Laurel St, Cannon Beach, OR 97110, USA

Closest City or Town: Cannon Beach, Oregon

How to Get There: Take US-101 N directly into Cannon Beach. The beach is centrally located within the town and is hard to miss!

GPS Coordinates: 45.8970300° N, 123.9638860° W

Best Time to Visit: Summer for warmer beach weather, though early fall offers stunning sunsets and fewer crowds.

Pass/Permit/Fees: No entrance fee to the beach.

Did You Know? Haystack Rock, visible from Cannon Beach, is one of the largest sea stacks on the Pacific Coast.

Website: https://www.cannonbeach.org/

Ecola State Park

Rediscover the wild, rugged beauty of Oregon's coastline at Ecola State Park. Nestled between the Pacific Ocean and the lush, green cliffs of the Oregon coast, this park offers a sweeping panorama that spans miles of undeveloped shoreline. Ideal for hikers, photographers, and nature lovers, the park's trails offer scenic views of the ocean, lighthouses, and possibly even migrating gray whales. Surfing and picnicking are also popular here, making it a versatile destination for all outdoor enthusiasts.

Location: Cannon Beach, OR 97110, USA

Closest City or Town: Cannon Beach, Oregon

How to Get There: Head north on Ecola Park Rd from downtown Cannon Beach; follow the signs to the park entrance.

GPS Coordinates: 45.9406128° N, 123.9861940° W

Best Time to Visit: Year-round, though summer provides the best weather for hiking and beach activities.

Pass/Permit/Fees: State park pass required; daily fees or annual pass available.

Did You Know? Ecola State Park has served as a filming location for several movies, including '"The Goonies"' and '"Point Break."'

Website:
https://stateparks.oregon.gov/index.cfm?do=park.profile&parkId=1
36

CASCADE LOCKS

Bonneville Lock & Dam

Explore the engineering marvel of the Bonneville Lock & Dam, situated in the scenic Columbia River Gorge. This historic dam plays a crucial role in powering homes and industries with its hydroelectric facility. Besides learning about its impressive functionality, visitors can revel in activities like salmon viewing at the fish ladders, taking guided tours of the powerhouses, or simply enjoying the surrounding natural beauty known for its spectacular waterfalls and abundant wildlife.

Location: Bonneville Dam, Cascade Locks, OR 97014, USA

Closest City or Town: Cascade Locks, Oregon

How to Get There: Take I-84 E from Portland to Exit 40. Follow signs directly to the dam.

GPS Coordinates: 45.6442837° N, 121.9406369° W

Best Time to Visit: Open year-round; spring and fall for witnessing fish migrations.

Pass/Permit/Fees: No entrance fee.

Did You Know? The dam's fish ladders are equipped with windows allowing visitors to watch migrating salmon and sturgeon.

Website: https://www.nwp.usace.army.mil/bonneville/

Bridge of the Gods

Cross the thrilling Bridge of the Gods, an awe-inspiring cantilever bridge that spans the majestic Columbia River. Connecting Oregon and Washington, this bridge offers unparalleled views of the river gorge, especially during sunrise or sunset. Consider a stop here while exploring nearby hiking trails or on a drive along the historic Columbia River Highway. It's a favorite spot not just for its views, but also for the legendary Native American lore that surrounds its name.

Location: Columbia River Gorge, Cascade Locks, OR 97014

Closest City or Town: Cascade Locks, Oregon

How to Get There: Follow I-84 to Cascade Locks and take Exit 44. Follow the signs to the bridge.

GPS Coordinates: 45.6623207° N, 121.9010507° W

Best Time to Visit: Accessible year-round, but particularly stunning in the fall when the foliage changes color.

Pass/Permit/Fees: Toll bridge; fee for crossing.

Did You Know? The bridge is named after a natural dam created by a landslide, believed in local Native American legend to be placed by the gods.

Website: http://portofcascadelocks.org/bridge-of-the-gods

Horsetail Falls Columbia River Gorge

Discover the enchanting Horsetail Falls, located in the heart of the Columbia River Gorge. This unique waterfall, shaped remarkably like a horsetail, plunges gracefully near the roadside, making it an easily accessible yet still breathtaking site. The area offers picnic spots and a short trailhead, leading to upper viewpoints and connecting to other waterfalls nearby for those seeking a more adventurous trek. It's an idyllic spot for nature lovers and those looking to escape into Oregon's wild beauty.

Location: Horsetail Falls, Oregon 97014, USA

Closest City or Town: Cascade Locks, Oregon

How to Get There: Located along the Historic Columbia River Highway, approximately 2.5 miles east of Multnomah Falls.

GPS Coordinates: 45.5896191° N, 122.0686650° W

Best Time to Visit: Spring to early fall for optimal waterfall flow and pleasant hiking weather.

Pass/Permit/Fees: No entrance fee.

Did You Know? Horsetail Falls is part of the famous Columbia River Gorge National Scenic Area, known for its dense concentrations of waterfalls.

Website:
https://www.fs.usda.gov/recarea/crgnsa/recarea/?recid=29934"

Columbia River Highway

Step back in time as you journey along the Columbia River Highway, a marvel of early 20th-century engineering draped in natural beauty. Winding along the mighty Columbia River, this historic route offers breathtaking views, mesmerizing waterfalls, and an unmatched glimpse into Oregon's lush landscapes. Imagine driving under canopies of green or stopping at panoramic viewpoints that offer dramatic vistas of the river gorge. It's not just a drive; it's a journey through Oregon's grandeur!

Location: Historic Columbia River Hwy, Oregon, USA

Closest City or Town: Portland, Oregon (just a short drive away)

How to Get There: From downtown Portland, take I-84 E towards Hood River. Exit on Troutdale, and follow the signs to the Historic Columbia River Highway.

GPS Coordinates: 45.5341203° N, 122.2323162° W

Best Time to Visit: Spring and early summer when the waterfalls are at their fullest and the wildflowers are in bloom.

Pass/Permit/Fees: No fees are required to drive the highway; however, some parks and recreation sites along the route may charge a parking fee.

Did You Know? The Columbia River Highway was the first planned scenic roadway in the United States, leading to its designation as a National Historic Landmark.

Website: https://www.oregon.gov/odot/regions/pages/historic-columbia-river-highway.aspx

CAVE JUNCTION

Oregon Caves National Monument and Preserve

Discover a hidden subterranean wonderland at Oregon Caves National Monument and Preserve. Deep within the Siskiyou Mountains, this intricate cave system invites the daring to explore its marble halls adorned with stalactites, stalagmites, and ancient rock formations. Above ground, the preserve paints a landscape of diverse wildlife and lush forest trails that promise serene hikes and moments of solitude.

Location: 19000 Caves Hwy, Cave Junction, OR 97523-9746

Closest City or Town: Grants Pass, Oregon

How to Get There: Drive south from Grants Pass along US-199, then turn off at Cave Junction following the signs for the cave.

GPS Coordinates: 42.0983039° N, 123.4070036° W

Best Time to Visit: Late spring to early fall for the best cave touring conditions.

Pass/Permit/Fees: Entrance fees apply for cave tours; other passes may be required for parking.

Did You Know? The caves were formed from marble dissolved by rainwater, creating one of the few marble caves in the world.

Website: http://www.nps.gov/orca/

Coos Bay

Shore Acres State Park

Embrace the rugged beauty of Oregon's coastline at Shore Acres State Park, where towering cliffs meet the roaring Pacific Ocean. This spectacular park is renowned for its lush gardens, dramatic shorelines, and migrating whales spotted off the coast. Whether you're strolling through the formal gardens or watching the sunset paint the waves, Shore Acres offers a stunning natural canvas that captivates all who visit.

Location: 89039 Cape Arago Hwy, Coos Bay, OR 97420

Closest City or Town: Coos Bay, Oregon

How to Get There: From Coos Bay, follow the Cape Arago Highway southwest for scenic access to the park.

GPS Coordinates: 43.3168729° N, 124.3844167° W

Best Time to Visit: Summer for garden blooms and winter for storm watching and whale migration.

Pass/Permit/Fees: State Park pass required; daily or annual passes available.

Did You Know? The park's land was once part of a grand estate owned by lumber baron Louis J. Simpson, who created the gardens.

Website: https://shoreacres.net/

Cape Arago State Park

Unleash your inner explorer at Cape Arago State Park, where secluded coves and pristine forests await. Located at the end of Cape Arago Highway, this hidden gem offers peace away from the crowds, with opportunities to view seals and sea lions on offshore rocks or walk the trails that fringe the rugged coastline. Perfect for a day of hiking, picnicking, and photography, Cape Arago is a sanctuary of tranquility and natural beauty.

Location: Cape Arago State Park, Cape Arago Hwy, Coos Bay, OR 97420, USA

Closest City or Town: Coos Bay, Oregon

How to Get There: Continue along Cape Arago Highway past Shore Acres State Park. The road ends at the state park.

GPS Coordinates: 43.3063127° N, 124.3986423° W

Best Time to Visit: Year-round, though summer offers the mildest weather for outdoor activities.

Pass/Permit/Fees: No entrance fees, but some areas may require a parking fee.

Did You Know? Cape Arago was originally named by Spanish explorers and has a rich history of Native American habitation.

Website:
https://stateparks.oregon.gov/index.cfm?do=park.profile&parkId=6 6

CORBETT

Vista House

Immerse yourself in history and panoramic views at Vista House. Perched atop Crown Point along the Historic Columbia River Highway, this octagonal stone building serves as both a memorial to pioneers and a comfort station for travelers. With its opulent marble interior and breathtaking overlooks, Vista House provides a unique vantage point to appreciate the grandeur of the Columbia Gorge and its scenic surroundings.

Location: 40700 E Historic Columbia River Hwy, Corbett, OR 97019-9725

Closest City or Town: Troutdale, Oregon

How to Get There: From Portland, head east on I-84, take Exit 22 to Corbett, and follow signs to the Historic Columbia River Highway and Vista House.

GPS Coordinates: 45.5395771° N, 122.2444619° W

Best Time to Visit: Spring through fall, when the weather is clear and the views are most spectacular.

Pass/Perit/Fees: No entrance fees required; donations are appreciated for maintenance and preservation.

Did You Know? Vista House was built in 1918 as a tribute to Oregon pioneers and as a place of rest for travelers on the historic highway.

Website: http://www.vistahouse.com/

Latourell Falls

Discover the sheer beauty of Oregon's natural landscapes at Latourell Falls, where water cascades dramatically over a 224-foot cliff, creating a breathtaking spectacle. This striking waterfall, known for its slender form and close proximity to the Columbia River Gorge, offers an outstanding scenic experience. Visitors can indulge in an easy hike that leads directly to the base of the falls, ensuring an up-close encounter with the roaring water and vibrant, lush surroundings.

Ideal for photography enthusiasts and nature lovers alike, Latourell Falls stands as a captivating highlight in the verdant Oregon landscape.

Location: Oregon 97019, USA

Closest City or Town: Troutdale, Oregon (a scenic drive away)

How to Get There: From Portland, head east on I-84 E to exit 28 for Bridal Veil, then follow the Historic Columbia River Highway to the Latourell Falls parking area.

GPS Coordinates: 45.5369979° N, 122.2177965° W

Best Time to Visit: Spring and early summer when the flow is strongest due to snowmelt.

Pass/Permit/Fees: Free; no pass required.

Did You Know? Latourell Falls is unique because of its basalt column backdrop, distinctly visible behind the cascade of water.

Website: https://en.wikipedia.org/wiki/Latourell_Falls

DAYTON

Domaine Serene Vineyards & Winery

Step into the world of fine wine at Domaine Serene Vineyards & Winery, set atop the picturesque hills of Dayton, Oregon. Renowned for its award-winning Pinot Noirs and Chardonnays, this winery offers a luxurious tasting experience amid the tranquil Willamette Valley. Visitors can tour the state-of-the-art facilities, stroll through the lush vineyards, and unwind at the elegant tasting room where the true essence of Oregon wine can be savored alongside breathtaking views. Domaine Serene is a testament to the richness of the region's wine culture and a must-visit for connoisseurs and novices alike.

Location: 6555 NE Hilltop Ln, Dayton, OR 97114-7227

Closest City or Town: McMinnville, Oregon

How to Get There: From McMinnville, take NE 3rd St and OR-99W N to NE Hilltop Ln in Yamhill County.

GPS Coordinates: 45.2704073° N, 123.0685637° W

Best Time to Visit: Late spring through fall for beautiful vineyard views and ideal weather.

Pass/Permit/Fees: Tasting fees apply; reservations recommended.

Did You Know? Domaine Serene's founders were inspired by the wine-making techniques of Burgundy, France.

Website: http://www.domaineserene.com/visit-us

DRAKE CROSSING

Silver Falls State Park

Escape into the wilderness at Silver Falls State Park, Oregon's largest state park, known as the "crown jewel" of the state park system. With its renowned Trail of Ten Falls, visitors can embark on a majestic hiking experience that offers an up-close view of no less than ten stunning waterfalls within a single loop. This park is not just about waterfalls; it offers over 35 miles of backcountry trails for hiking, mountain biking, and horseback riding through dense forests and broad meadows. Silver Falls State Park epitomizes the adventure and natural beauty of Oregon.

Location: 725 Summer Street NE, Drake Crossing, OR 97301

Closest City or Town: Silverton, Oregon

How to Get There: From Silverton, head south on OR-214 S/Cascade Highway toward Drake Crossing.

GPS Coordinates: 44.9448775° N, 123.0281179° W

Best Time to Visit: Spring for high water levels and vibrant greenery or fall for colorful foliage.

Pass/Permit/Fees: State Park Pass required; day-use fee at the park entrance.

Did You Know? Silver Falls State Park was almost turned into a national park in the 1920s because of its stunning beauty.

Website: http://www.oregonstateparks.org/park_211.php

EUGENE

Cascades Raptor Center

Discover the thrilling world of birds of prey at the Cascades Raptor Center in Eugene, Oregon. Nestled on a wooded hillside, this nature center and wildlife hospital is dedicated to the rehabilitation and release of injured raptors, offering visitors an extraordinary opportunity to learn about and observe these magnificent birds up close. The center houses one of the largest collections of native raptor species in the Pacific Northwest, making it a fascinating educational experience for all ages. Engage with the natural world in an intimate and inspiring setting at the Cascades Raptor Center.

Location: 32275 Fox Hollow Rd, Eugene, OR 97405-9505

Closest City or Town: Eugene, Oregon

How to Get There: From downtown Eugene, take OR-126 W. Exit onto Fox Hollow Rd and follow the signs to the center.

GPS Coordinates: 43.9869780° N, 123.0787930° W

Best Time to Visit: Open year-round, but spring through fall offers the most pleasant weather for visiting.

Pass/Permit/Fees: Entrance fees required; membership options available.

Did You Know? The center not only rehabilitates birds but also focuses on public education regarding the ecological roles of raptors.

Website: http://cascadesraptorcenter.org/

Willamette River Bike Trail

Embark on a scenic cycling adventure along the Willamette River Bike Trail, a well-loved route that offers spectacular views of Oregon's lush landscape and the gently flowing Willamette River. Stretching through various parks and natural areas, this extensive trail is perfect for cyclists and pedestrians alike, featuring both paved and dirt paths suitable for all skill levels. Whether you're in for a short ride or a long-distance exploration, the Willamette River Bike Trail offers a refreshing outdoor experience, connecting you with nature and the vibrant communities along the river.

Location: Willamette River, Oregon, USA

Closest City or Town: Eugene, Oregon

How to Get There: Access the trail from multiple points; downtown Eugene is a great starting point.

GPS Coordinates: 44.8379206° N, 122.9361871° W

Best Time to Visit: Year-round accessibility, with spring and fall providing especially pleasant riding conditions.

Pass/Permit/Fees: Free; no pass required.

Did You Know? The trail is part of a larger network that plans to extend along the Willamette River for over 200 miles.

Website:
https://stateparks.oregon.gov/index.cfm?do=park.profile&parkId=2
17

King Estate Winery

Savor the essence of Oregon's renowned wine culture at King Estate Winery, a beacon of biodynamic vineyard practices nestled in the rolling hills near Eugene. This sprawling estate is not just a winery; it's a culinary journey. Imagine sipping on a glass of their flagship Pinot Noir while gazing out over the lush Willamette Valley. The winery offers tours that elucidate their organic farming methods and the craftsmanship behind their award-winning wines. The elegant on-site restaurant complements your wine-tasting experience with dishes that feature organic ingredients grown right on the estate.

Location: 80854 Territorial Hwy, Eugene, OR 97405-9715

Closest City or Town: Eugene, Oregon

How to Get There: Drive south from Eugene on OR-99W. Turn left onto Bailey Hill Road, then right onto Territorial Hwy. The winery is on the right after about 12 miles.

GPS Coordinates: 43.8609479° N, 123.2506801° W

Best Time to Visit: Summer for the best vineyard views and wine-tasting on sunny terraces.

Pass/Permit/Fees: Free entry; wine-tasting fees vary.

Did You Know? King Estate is the largest biodynamic vineyard in North America.

Website: http://www.kingestate.com/

University of Oregon

Plunge into the dynamic world of academia at the University of Oregon, located in the vibrant city of Eugene. The university is renowned for its commitment to education, research, and sports. Walk through the historic campus where lush greenery surrounds Gothic-style buildings, breathe in the intellectual atmosphere, and perhaps catch a thrilling Ducks football game. Don't miss the Jordan Schnitzer Museum of Art and the Museum of Natural and Cultural History, both located on campus, offering a dive into art and heritage without stepping off university grounds.

Location: 1585 E 13th Ave., Eugene, OR 97403

Closest City or Town: Eugene, Oregon

How to Get There: Located in downtown Eugene, easily accessible via Franklin Blvd with parking on campus available.

GPS Coordinates: 44.0448302° N, 123.0726055° W

Best Time to Visit: Spring and fall when the campus is buzzing with student activities.

Pass/Permit/Fees: Campus tours are free, but some museums may charge a small admission fee.

Did You Know? This university is where Nike founder Phil Knight and his coach Bill Bowerman initiated their shoe-making experiments.

Website: http://www.uoregon.edu/

Eugene Saturday Market

Experience the vibrant pulse of local creativity at the Eugene Saturday Market, Oregon's weekly mosaic of culture, crafts, and cuisine. Every Saturday, the heart of downtown Eugene transforms into a bustling marketplace where local artisans, chefs, and musicians share their talents with the community. From unique handcrafted jewelry to gourmet street food and live entertainment, this market invites visitors to immerse themselves in the lively spirit of Eugene. It's more than a market; it's a celebration of all things locally produced and an inviting community gathering.

Location: 126 E. 8th Avenue, Eugene, OR 97401

Closest City or Town: Eugene, Oregon

How to Get There: Located in downtown Eugene, accessible by all major bus lines serving the area. Parking is available in surrounding public parking structures.

GPS Coordinates: 44.0506443° N, 123.0918372° W

Best Time to Visit: Saturdays, especially from April through November, when the market is in full swing.

Pass/Permit/Fees: Free to visit.

Did You Know? The Eugene Saturday Market has been a vital part of the community since 1970, making it the longest-running weekly market in the United States.

Website:https://www.eugene-or.gov/4574/Downtown-Events-Schedule

FLORENCE

Sea Lion Caves

Explore the rugged Oregon coastline's natural wonder at Sea Lion Caves, America's largest sea cave and year-round home to wild sea lions. Nestled just north of Florence, this natural sanctuary offers visitors a unique opportunity to observe sea lions in their natural habitat through a viewing area built into the cavern's rock. Listen to the barking of Steller sea lions, watch as they frolic and lounge, and soak in the breathtaking ocean views that stretch out into infinity from this vantage point.

Location: 91560 Highway 101, Florence, OR 97439-8233

Closest City or Town: Florence, Oregon

How to Get There: Take Highway 101 north from Florence for 11 miles. The caves are on the ocean side of the highway.

GPS Coordinates: 44.1217581° N, 124.1267426° W

Best Time to Visit: Visit in fall and winter to see the most significant number of sea lions.

Pass/Permit/Fees: Admission fee required; check website for current pricing.

Did You Know? The cave system was formed over 25 million years ago and discovered in 1880 by a local seaman.

Website: http://www.sealioncaves.com/

Heceta Head Lighthouse

Venture to Heceta Head Lighthouse, perched on a cliff along the beautiful Oregon coast, offering panoramic views and a peek into maritime history. This iconic lighthouse, dating back to 1894, is listed on the National Register of Historic Places. Visitors can tour the lighthouse, explore the keeper's house, and enjoy trails that lead through old-growth forests to spectacular ocean overlooks. The surrounding area serves as a habitat for various wildlife, including seabirds and, occasionally, passing whales.

Location: 92072 Highway 101, Florence, OR 97439-8234

Closest City or Town: Florence, Oregon

How to Get There: Take Highway 101 north from Florence for approximately 14 miles. The lighthouse is well-signposted.

GPS Coordinates: 44.1373833° N, 124.1281066° W

Best Time to Visit: Summer for the best weather and migratory whale watching in winter.

Pass/Permit/Fees: Parking fee required; lighthouse tour may have a separate fee.

Did You Know? Heceta Head Lighthouse emits the strongest light on the Oregon coast, visible up to 21 miles out to sea.

Website: http://hecetalighthouse.com/"

Jessie M. Honeyman Memorial State Park

Discover a sanctuary of sand and forest adventures at Jessie M. Honeyman Memorial State Park, a gem nestled between the ocean dunes and wooded areas of Florence, Oregon. Perfect for campers and outdoor enthusiasts, this park offers a variety of activities including hiking, sandboarding, and swimming in two freshwater lakes. Explore the second largest Oregon state park, which provides a picturesque setting for picnicking and dune buggy rides among majestic coastal scenery. A highlight is the opportunity to glide down the vast sand dunes or kayak in peaceful lake waters.

Location: 84505 Highway 101, Florence, OR 97439-8405

Closest City or Town: Florence, Oregon

How to Get There: From Florence, drive south on Highway 101 for about three miles; the park entrance will be well-marked on your left.

GPS Coordinates: 43.9290983° N, 124.1054538° W

Best Time to Visit: Summer for the best weather and full access to all park amenities

Pass/Permit/Fees: Day-use parking fee; additional fees for camping and certain activities

Did You Know? This park is named after Jessie M. Honeyman, a local businesswoman dedicated to the preservation of Oregon's natural beauty.

Website:http://www.oregonstateparks.org/index.cfm?do=parkPage .dsp_parkPage&parkId=95

GOVERNMENT CAMP

Trillium Lake

Escape to the serene beauty of Trillium Lake, situated a short distance from Government Camp, Oregon. This idyllic spot offers breathtaking views of Mount Hood reflecting on its calm waters, especially enchanting at sunrise or sunset. Trillium Lake is renowned for its accessible fishing, swimming, and scenic hiking trails that encircle the lake, providing splendid photo opportunities. The area is a popular destination for picnics and canoeing, offering a tranquil retreat from the bustling city life.

Location: National Forest Development Road 2612, Government Camp, OR 97028

Closest City or Town: Government Camp, Oregon

How to Get There: Take US-26 E to Timberline Rd in Government Camp, then follow signs to Trillium Lake on Forest Road 2612.

GPS Coordinates: 45.2683925° N, 121.7387987° W

Best Time to Visit: Late spring through early fall for the most pleasant weather

Pass/Permit/Fees: A Northwest Forest Pass is required for parking.

Did You Know? The lake was artificially created during the construction of the Timberline Lodge and is named after the Trillium flower, commonly seen in the area.

Website:https://www.recreation.gov/recreationalAreaDetails.do?contractCode=NRSO&parkId=252467&facilityId=252467&agencyCode=70903

Timberline Lodge

Step into a historical masterpiece at Timberline Lodge, located high on the slopes of Mount Hood. This National Historic Landmark, constructed during the Great Depression through a New Deal program, boasts rustic architecture and is a haven for ski enthusiasts with its year-round snow. The lodge is not just for skiers; visitors can enjoy fine dining with a view, explore the rich history displayed throughout the establishment, or simply unwind by the grand fireplace, a perfect blend of relaxation and adventure.

Location: 27500 E Timberline Rd, Government Camp, OR 97028

Closest City or Town: Government Camp, Oregon

How to Get There: From Portland, take US-26 E directly to Timberline Lodge Road and follow the signs leading to the lodge.

GPS Coordinates: 45.3311281° N, 121.7110064° W

Best Time to Visit: Winter for skiing, summer for hiking and sightseeing

Pass/Permit/Fees: No entrance fee; fees for lodging and other services vary

Did You Know? Timberline Lodge served as the exterior of the Overlook Hotel in the iconic horror film '"The Shining.'"

Website: http://www.timberlinelodge.com/

Timberline Lodge Ski Area

Ascend to the snowy heights of Timberline Lodge Ski Area, where the spirit of winter sports is alive throughout the year. Renowned for its historical lodge and year-round skiing on the slopes of Mount Hood, Timberline offers a unique mountain experience with breathtaking views and runs for all skill levels. Whether you're carving down advanced trails or enjoying a cozy retreat by the fire, the rustic charm of Timberline Lodge awaits.

Location: Mt. Hood National Forest Timberline Lodge, Government Camp, OR 97028

Closest City or Town: Government Camp, Oregon

How to Get There: Drive east from Portland on US-26 E. Turn right onto OR-173 E/Woodlands Rd and continue to Timberline Rd.

GPS Coordinates: 45.3140631° N, 121.7262328° W

Best Time to Visit: Year-round skiing available, with summer offering unique alpine hiking opportunities.

Pass/Permit/Fees: Lift ticket prices vary; check the website for current rates.

Did You Know? The iconic lodge was used as the exterior of the Overlook Hotel in the film '"The Shining."'

Website: https://www.timberlinelodge.com/mountain/ski-area

GRANTS PASS

Wildlife Images Rehabilitation & Education Center

Immerse yourself in the world of wildlife conservation at Wildlife Images Rehabilitation & Education Center in Grants Pass, Oregon. This non-profit sanctuary focuses on the care and rehabilitation of injured and orphaned wildlife, offering guided tours where visitors can learn about wildlife rescue and recovery. Engage with various animals through educational programs and see firsthand the efforts made to return them to their natural habitats.

Location: 11845 Lower River Rd, Grants Pass, OR 97526-9613

Closest City or Town: Grants Pass, Oregon

How to Get There: From Grants Pass, head southwest on Lower River Road for about 12 miles; the center is on the right.

GPS Coordinates: 42.4902431° N, 123.4741756° W

Best Time to Visit: Spring and summer for the best weather and active wildlife

Pass/Permit/Fees: Admission fees apply; check website for current rates

Did You Know? The center offers a unique "'Animal Encounters'" program, allowing visitors to get up close with some of the resident animals.

Website: http://www.wildlifeimages.org/

The Glass Forge

Venture into the fiery heart of creativity at The Glass Forge in Grants Pass, Oregon. This artisan studio specializes in the mesmerizing art of glassblowing. Visitors can watch skilled artisans shape molten glass into beautiful artwork or even participate in hands-on workshops to create their own glass pieces. The gallery showcases a variety of glass art, making it an ideal spot for finding unique gifts or gaining inspiration for your own creative endeavors.

Location: 501 SW G St, Grants Pass, OR 97526-2472

Closest City or Town: Grants Pass, Oregon

How to Get There: Located in downtown Grants Pass, easily accessible from Interstate 5 via exit 58, following signs to the city center.

GPS Coordinates: 42.4399987° N, 123.3311378° W

Best Time to Visit: Year-round; check for special events and workshops

Pass/Permit/Fees: No admission fee for demonstrations; workshops and classes vary in price

Did You Know? The Glass Forge often hosts live demonstrations and classes, allowing guests to engage directly with the glassblowing process.

Website: http://glassforge.com/

HAMMOND

Fort Stevens State Park

Experience history and nature intertwined at Fort Stevens State Park, where the whispers of the past meet the tranquility of the ocean. This historic site, once an active military fort, offers a rare chance to explore a shipwreck, the Peter Iredale, grounded since 1906. Wander through old military batteries, watch for wildlife, and stroll along the sandy shores that stretch as far as the eye can see.

Location: 1675 Peter Iredale Rd, Hammond, OR 97121

Closest City or Town: Astoria, Oregon

How to Get There: From Astoria, head west on US-101 S, follow signs for Fort Stevens State Park.

GPS Coordinates: 46.1825287° N, 123.9616688° W

Best Time to Visit: Summer for the best weather, though spring and fall are great for fewer crowds.

Pass/Permit/Fees: $5 daily vehicle fee or state park pass required.

Did You Know? Fort Stevens was in operation from the Civil War through World War II, making it one of the most enduring fortifications in the U.S.

Website:http://www.oregonstateparks.org/index.cfm?do=parkPage .dsp_parkPage&parkId=129

HOOD RIVER

Western Antique Aeroplane & Automobile Museum

Soar into the past at the Western Antique Aeroplane & Automobile Museum in Hood River, where history takes flight. This museum is a haven for aviation and auto enthusiasts, featuring one of the largest collections of still-operational antique aeroplanes and automobiles in the country. Experience the thrills of yesteryears through guided tours, demonstrations, and special events that bring these classic machines to life.

Location: 1600 Air Museum Rd, Hood River, OR 97031-9800

Closest City or Town: Hood River, Oregon

How to Get There: Take I-84, exit 62 for US-30 W towards West Hood River. Follow signs to the museum.

GPS Coordinates: 45.6768599° N, 121.5412344° W

Best Time to Visit: Spring through fall, with special events often in summer.

Pass/Permit/Fees: Entrance fees apply; see website for details.

Did You Know? Many of the planes and vehicles in the museum's collection are still used in flying and driving events.

Website: http://www.waaamuseum.org/

JOSEPH

Wallowa Lake Tramway

Ascend to new heights on the Wallowa Lake Tramway, Oregon's gateway to the breathtaking peaks of the Wallowa Mountains. This aerial journey gifts visitors with stunning panoramic views as they rise to the summit of Mount Howard. Upon reaching the top, immerse yourself in nature through hiking trails or enjoy a meal with a view at the mountain-top restaurant.

Location: 59919 Wallowa Lake Hwy, Joseph, OR 97846-8334

Closest City or Town: Joseph, Oregon

How to Get There: From Joseph, head south on OR-351 toward Wallowa Lake; the tramway is near the end of the highway.

GPS Coordinates: 45.2762020° N, 117.2057510° W

Best Time to Visit: Summer for aerial rides and winter for snow sports.

Pass/Permit/Fees: Tickets required for tram rides; prices available on the website.

Did You Know? The tram reaches heights of nearly 4,000 feet, making it one of the highest in North America.

Website: http://www.wallowalaketramway.com/index.html

LINCOLN CITY

Lincoln City Glass Center

Ignite your creativity at the Lincoln City Glass Center, a glowing corner of Oregon where visitors can shape their very own glass art. Under the guidance of expert glassblowers, participate in the fascinating process of glass-making. Whether crafting a colorful float, a unique vase, or another glass treasure, the center offers a hands-on experience that sparks joy and creativity.

Location: 4821 SW Highway Suite 101, Lincoln City, OR 97367

Closest City or Town: Lincoln City, Oregon

How to Get There: Located along the Oregon Coast Highway (US-101), easily accessible from central Lincoln City.

GPS Coordinates: 44.9292804° N, 124.0169250° W

Best Time to Visit: Year-round, though warmer months are perfect for visiting the coast.

Pass/Permit/Fees: Charges for glass-making sessions vary; pre-booking recommended.

Did You Know? Each piece created by visitors is a unique work of art, as no two glassblowing sessions are the same.

Website: http://www.lincolncityglasscenter.com/

Lincoln City Outlets

Unleash your inner shopper at the Lincoln City Outlets, a premier coastal shopping destination in Oregon. With a variety of stores offering everything from high-end brands to unique local goods, this outlet mall ensures an enjoyable hunt for bargains amidst the scenic beauty of the Pacific Northwest coast. The pleasant, open-air layout invites you to stroll and shop at your leisure.

Location: 1500 SE East Devils Lake Rd, Lincoln City, OR 97367-2660

Closest City or Town: Lincoln City, Oregon

How to Get There: Directly accessible from US-101, this shopping destination is easy to find in the heart of Lincoln City.

GPS Coordinates: 44.9588910° N, 124.0112237° W

Best Time to Visit: Year-round attraction, with special sales during major holidays.

Pass/Permit/Fees: Free to visit; shopping costs vary by store and sales events.

Did You Know? The outlet is known for its coastal wind-themed architecture, reflecting the natural environment of Lincoln City.

Website: http://www.lincolncityoutlets.com/

MANZANITA

Manzanita Beach

Discover the rugged charm of Manzanita Beach, a hidden gem along the Oregon coast. With its expansive sandy shores framed by the dramatic Neahkahnie Mountain, it provides an idyllic escape for nature lovers and photographers alike. Located in the quaint town of Manzanita, this beach is a perfect blend of tranquility and natural beauty, offering activities from surfing and kite flying to leisurely beach walks. Its unspoiled landscape is particularly enchanting at sunset when the sky casts vibrant hues over the Pacific Ocean.

Location: Manzanita, OR, USA

Closest City or Town: Manzanita

How to Get There: From Portland, follow US-26 W to OR-53 S in Necanicum Junction. Continue on OR-53 S. Drive to Manzanita Ave.

GPS Coordinates: 45.7199821° N, 123.9406300° W

Best Time to Visit: Summer for warm weather or fall for dramatic storm watching.

Pass/Permit/Fees: Free access to the public.

Did You Know? Manzanita means ""little apple"" in Spanish, named for the small, crabapple-like fruit found in the area.

Website: https://en.wikipedia.org/wiki/Manzanita,_Oregon

McMINNVILLE

Evergreen Aviation & Space Museum

Step into the world of aerial innovation at the Evergreen Aviation & Space Museum, home to the famous Hughes H-4 Hercules '"Spruce Goose."' This museum in McMinnville serves as a playground for aviation enthusiasts, showcasing a vast array of aircraft and spacecraft that chart the evolution of airborne and space technology. Visitors can explore exhibits that range from World War II bombers to modern unmanned aerial vehicles, offering a comprehensive view of the history and future of flight.

Location: 500 NE Captain Michael King Smith Way, McMinnville, OR 97128-8877

Closest City or Town: McMinnville

How to Get There: Take OR-99W S from Portland, and follow signs to the museum entrance.

GPS Coordinates: 45.2043040° N, 123.1454300° W

Best Time to Visit: Year-round, with indoor exhibits perfect for any weather.

Pass/Permit/Fees: Entry fees apply; check the website for current pricing.

Did You Know? The '"Spruce Goose"' is the largest wooden airplane ever constructed and was flown only once.

Website: http://www.evergreenmuseum.org/

MEDFORD

Rogue River

Embark on an exhilarating outdoor adventure along the Rogue River, a vital waterway in southwestern Oregon known for its thrilling whitewater rafting. Winding through the lush Siskiyou National Forest near Medford, the river offers a paradise for anglers, rafters, and nature enthusiasts. From serene floats to Class IV rapids, the Rogue River caters to all levels of rafting experience, surrounded by a scenic backdrop that enhances the sense of wilderness and escape.

Location: 3040 Biddle Road Siskiyou National Forest, Medford, OR 97504

Closest City or Town: Medford

How to Get There: From Medford, take I-5 S and exit for Merlin. Follow Merlin-Galice Rd to the river access points.

GPS Coordinates: 42.3620183° N, 122.8748342° W

Best Time to Visit: Late spring through early fall for rafting; year-round for fishing.

Pass/Permit/Fees: Various permits may be required for fishing and rafting; check local regulations.

Did You Know? The Rogue River was one of the original eight rivers included in the Wild and Scenic Rivers Act of 1968.

Website: http://www.fs.usda.gov/rogue-siskiyou/

MITCHELL

John Day Fossil Beds National Monument

Venture back in time at John Day Fossil Beds National Monument, where the rich tapestry of Oregon's ecological and geological history is captured in colorful rock formations and well-preserved fossils. Located near Mitchell, Oregon, this monumental area is divided into three units, each featuring unique aspects of past climates and ecosystems that once thrived in the region. Visitors can explore the Painted Hills Unit for its striking landscapes, or delve into ancient life at the Thomas Condon Paleontology Center.

Location: 32651 OR-19, Mitchell, OR 97750, USA

Closest City or Town: Mitchell

How to Get There: From Bend, take US-20 E to OR-19 N, directly leading to the monument.

GPS Coordinates: 44.5634640° N, 119.6483760° W

Best Time to Visit: Spring and fall for mild weather and optimal viewing conditions.

Pass/Permit/Fees: No entrance fees.

Did You Know? The monument's fossils represent nearly 40 million years of plant and animal evolution.

Website: https://www.nps.gov/joda/

MT HOOD

Mount Hood

Ascend the iconic Mount Hood, Oregon's highest peak, and a beacon for outdoor enthusiasts. This majestic mountain offers year-round recreational activities, from premier skiing and snowboarding in the winter to scenic hiking and camping during the warmer months. Its slopes are dotted with diverse ecosystems and panoramic views that attract adventurers and nature lovers from around the world. Whether you seek a challenging climb or a peaceful retreat in the alpine forests, Mount Hood provides an unforgettable backdrop for outdoor exploration.

Location: Mt Hood, OR 97041, USA

Closest City or Town: Government Camp

How to Get There: From Portland, take US-26 E directly to the Mount Hood area.

GPS Coordinates: 45.3736150° N, 121.6959510° W

Best Time to Visit: Winter for snow sports; summer for hiking and sightseeing.

Pass/Permit/Fees: Various passes required for national forest access and activities; check the website for details.

Did You Know? Mount Hood is considered one of Oregon's most likely volcanoes to erupt, though it has remained quiet for centuries.

Website: https://www.fs.usda.gov/mthood"

Crater Lake

Experience the awe-inspiring beauty of Crater Lake, a breathtaking natural wonder nestled in the heart of Oregon. Known for its vibrant blue color and stunning clarity, this lake was formed from a collapsed volcano, creating a mesmerizing landscape that captivates visitors year-round. Engage in activities like hiking, photography, and seasonal boat tours on the lake itself, each offering a unique perspective of this geological marvel. The park's Rim Drive offers panoramic views that are especially golden at sunrise and sunset, providing unforgettable sights and an ideal backdrop for nature lovers.

Location: Oregon 97604, USA

Closest City or Town: Klamath Falls, OR

How to Get There: From Klamath Falls, take OR-62 W and follow signs for Crater Lake National Park.

GPS Coordinates: 42.9445872° N, 122.1090039° W

Best Time to Visit: Summer for roads and facilities fully accessible; winter for spectacular snowy views.

Pass/Permit/Fees: Entrance fee required; check latest rates on website.

Did You Know? Crater Lake is the deepest lake in the United States and is considered one of the clearest and purest bodies of water in the world.

Website: https://www.nps.gov/crla/

NEWPORT

Oregon Coast Aquarium

Dive into the enchanting underwater world at the Oregon Coast Aquarium in Newport. This globally renowned facility not only showcases local marine life but also offers interactive experiences like shark encounters and sea otter feedings. Walk through the impressive Passages of the Deep tunnel, where you can be surrounded by sharks, rays, and colorful fish. Ideal for families and marine enthusiasts, this aquarium educates and inspires conservation through close-up encounters with nature's marine wonders.

Location: 2820 SE Ferry Slip Rd, Newport, OR 97365-5269

Closest City or Town: Newport, OR

How to Get There: From downtown Newport, head south on SE Ferry Slip Rd towards the Oregon Coast Aquarium signs.

GPS Coordinates: 44.6176528° N, 124.0472528° W

Best Time to Visit: Year-round, with feeding times and special events offering an enhanced experience.

Pass/Permit/Fees: Admission fee required; details on pricing are available on the aquarium's website.

Did You Know? The Oregon Coast Aquarium was once home to Keiko, the famous orca from the movie ""Free Willy.""

Website: http://aquarium.org/

Yaquina Head Outstanding Natural Area

Immerse yourself in the rugged beauty of Yaquina Head Outstanding Natural Area, where the historic Yaquina Head Lighthouse stands as Oregon's tallest lighthouse. Explore tide pools teeming with marine life, scenic trails, and birdwatching opportunities which make this spot a paradise for nature and wildlife enthusiasts. The interpretive center offers engaging exhibits about the area's natural and cultural history, perfect for enriching any visit.

Location: 750 NW Lighthouse Dr, Newport, OR 97365-1347

Closest City or Town: Newport, OR

How to Get There: Follow US-101 to NW Lighthouse Drive in Newport, marked by signs for Yaquina Head.

GPS Coordinates: 44.6762003° N, 124.0772211° W

Best Time to Visit: Year-round but particularly stunning from spring through fall.

Pass/Permit/Fees: Entry fee required; passes available at the site.

Did You Know? The Yaquina Head Lighthouse has been guiding ships since 1873 and is listed on the National Register of Historic Places.

Website: http://www.blm.gov/learn/interpretive-centers/yaquina

Yaquina Bay Lighthouse

Step back in time at Yaquina Bay Lighthouse, an iconic structure in Newport that offers a glimpse into Oregon's maritime history. This is the only existing Oregon lighthouse with the living quarters attached, and it is furnished in a 19th-century style, providing a feel for the era. Explore the small, charming museum within and enjoy the panoramic views of Yaquina Bay and the surrounding natural beauty.

Location: Yaquina Bay Lighthouse, Newport, OR 97365, USA

Closest City or Town: Newport, OR

How to Get There: From Newport, head south on US-101. Follow signs for the Historic Bayfront, then follow signs to the lighthouse.

GPS Coordinates: 44.6241361° N, 124.0630602° W

Best Time to Visit: Open year-round, but best visited during the less crowded spring and fall seasons.

Pass/Permit/Fees: No entrance fee; donations are accepted.

Did You Know? The lighthouse was decommissioned just three years after it was first lit in 1871.

Website: https://www.yaquinalights.org/

Devils Punchbowl State Natural Area

Witness the dramatic natural forces at play at Devils Punchbowl State Natural Area, where a hollow rock formation shaped like a giant punchbowl fills with tumultuous ocean waters. This natural spectacle, formed by the collapse of two sea caves, offers visitors a unique geological insight as well as a fantastic spot for whale watching during migration seasons. Nearby, sandy beaches and walking trails provide plenty of opportunities for hiking and beachcombing.

Location: US Highway 101 Otter Crest Loop, Newport, OR 97369

Closest City or Town: Newport, OR

How to Get There: Located off US Highway 101 on Otter Crest Loop, this area is well-signed and accessible by car.

GPS Coordinates: 44.7468595° N, 124.0635012° W

Best Time to Visit: Accessible year-round, with winter and spring being prime whale watching seasons.

Pass/Permit/Fees: No entrance fees.

Did You Know? The park is named after its resemblance to a large punch bowl.

Website:
http://www.oregonstateparks.org/index.cfm?do=parkPage.dsp_par kPage&parkId=156"

Nye Beach

Discover the charm and nostalgic beauty of Nye Beach, a beloved seaside enclave with a vibrant arts scene and a rich history dating back over a century. Situated in Newport, Oregon, this neighborhood offers a picturesque beachfront perfect for strolls, flying kites, and dipping your toes in the Pacific. Visitors can explore quaint bookstores, cozy cafes, and local galleries. Unique to Nye Beach is its community feel, enhanced by frequent cultural events and a welcoming local population that makes every visitor feel like a part of the community.

Location: Newport, OR 97365, USA

Closest City or Town: Newport, Oregon

How to Get There: From the center of Newport, head west towards the ocean on NW 3rd St until you reach the Nye Beach archway, signaling your arrival at this charming destination.

GPS Coordinates: 44.6423390° N, 124.0623396° W

Best Time to Visit: Summer for sunny beach days or fall for quieter visits and stunning sunsets.

Pass/Permit/Fees: Free access to the beach and town.

Did You Know? Nye Beach was a prime vacation destination in the 1900s, known as the "'Queen of Oregon Beaches.'"

Website: https://nyebeach.net/

Hatfield Marine Science Center

Immerse yourself in the wonders of marine life at the Hatfield Marine Science Center, a hub of research and education in Newport, Oregon. This engaging facility offers hands-on exhibits, aquariums, and educational programs that highlight marine biodiversity and conservation. It's a place where science comes alive, allowing visitors of all ages to explore the complexities of coastal environments. The center, part of Oregon State University, plays a crucial role in marine research on the Pacific Coast.

Location: 2030 SE Marine Science Drive, Newport, OR 97365-5296

Closest City or Town: Newport, Oregon

How to Get There: Take the US-101 to SE Marine Science Dr. The center is located just east of the Oregon Coast Aquarium.

GPS Coordinates: 44.6215492° N, 124.0464783° W

Best Time to Visit: Open year-round, but spring and summer offer additional programs.

Pass/Permit/Fees: Suggested donation for entry.

Did You Know? The center conducts groundbreaking research on tsunami preparedness along the Oregon coast.

Website: http://hmsc.oregonstate.edu/

Yaquina Bay Bridge

Marvel at the architectural elegance of the Yaquina Bay Bridge, an iconic Art Deco structure that spans Newport's Yaquina Bay. Opened in 1936, this historic bridge was designed by Conde McCullough and is a masterpiece of engineering and design, providing stunning views of the bay and the Pacific Ocean. Driving or walking across the bridge offers a panoramic experience of the ocean juxtaposed against the rugged coastal scenery. The bridge is not only a critical transportation link but also a beloved landmark in Newport.

Location: 1950 SW Coast Hwy, Newport, OR 97365, USA

Closest City or Town: Newport, Oregon

How to Get There: Accessible directly via US-101, the main coastal highway running through Newport.

GPS Coordinates: 44.6221832° N, 124.0564970° W

Best Time to Visit: Enjoyable year-round, with less foggy conditions typically in summer and early fall.

Pass/Permit/Fees: No fees to cross or view the bridge.

Did You Know? The Yaquina Bay Bridge was a part of the New Deal's infrastructure projects aimed at improving America's roads and national employment during the Great Depression.

Website: https://en.wikipedia.org/wiki/Yaquina_Bay_Bridge

South Beach State Park

Escape to the expansive sands and whispering waves of South Beach State Park, nestled just south of the Yaquina Bay Bridge in Newport. This park offers a plethora of outdoor activities, including camping, hiking, and biking on well-maintained trails, and beachcombing along miles of unspoiled shoreline. The park's Jetty Trail provides spectacular views and a direct route to the ocean. It's a favorite spot for kite flying, surf fishing, and picnicking, making it an ideal location for a family day out or a serene retreat.

Location: 5580 N Coast Hwy, Newport, OR 97365-1147

Closest City or Town: Newport, Oregon

How to Get There: South of the Yaquina Bay Bridge on US-101, follow signs for the park entrance.

GPS Coordinates: 44.6040432° N, 124.0615563° W

Best Time to Visit: Summer for beach activities; year-round for hiking and camping.

Pass/Permit/Fees: Day-use and camping fees apply.

Did You Know? South Beach State Park was established in the 1930s and has since been a popular coastal getaway.

Website:
http://oregonstateparks.org/index.cfm?do=parkPage.dsp_parkPage&parkId=149

OTTER ROCK

Otter Crest Loop

Venture off the beaten path and onto Otter Crest Loop, a scenic bypass that offers some of the most breathtaking views along the Oregon Coast. This less-traveled road winds through lush forests and opens up to vistas of rugged cliffs and the vast ocean. Perfect for a leisurely drive or a cycling adventure, spots like the Devil's Punchbowl and Cape Foulweather provide dramatic overlooks for photography and nature gazing. It's a journey that connects you deeply with the natural beauty of Oregon's coastal landscape.

Location: Oregon, USA

Closest City or Town: Newport, Oregon

How to Get There: From Newport, head north on US-101 and follow the signs to Otter Crest Loop just north of the Yaquina Head.

GPS Coordinates: 44.7631712° N, 124.0638843° W

Best Time to Visit: Late spring through early fall for the clearest skies and best road conditions.

Pass/Permit/Fees: No fees required to drive the loop.

Did You Know? Otter Crest Loop includes the highest point accessible by car along the Oregon coast, offering unmatched views of the Pacific.

Website: https://www.whalecoveinn.com/our-blog/guide-to-otter-crest-loop/

PACIFIC CITY

Pelican Brewing Company

Quench your thirst for coastal views and exceptional brews at Pelican Brewing Company, nestled on the pristine shores of Pacific City. As pioneers in the Oregon craft brewing scene, this brewery blends quality ingredients with the wild, oceanic backdrop it calls home. Whether you are sipping their award-winning beers or dining from their delicious menu, each experience is infused with the essence of the Pacific Northwest. Unwind on their beachfront patio where the sound of waves complements your craft beer experience.

Location: 33180 Cape Kiwanda Dr, Pacific City, OR 97135-8012

Closest City or Town: Pacific City

How to Get There: From Portland, take US-101 S to Pacific City exit. Follow signs to Cape Kiwanda Dr.

GPS Coordinates: 45.215143° N, 123.9705391° W

Best Time to Visit: Summer for the best beachside seating

Pass/Permit/Fees: No entrance fee, prices for beer and food vary

Did You Know? Pelican Brewing Company was the first beachfront brewpub in the Pacific Northwest.

Website: http://pelicanbrewing.com/

Cape Kiwanda State Natural Area

Escape to the dynamic landscape of Cape Kiwanda State Natural Area, where the power of the ocean meets the tranquility of the sand dunes. Located in Pacific City, this natural playground offers activities like sandboarding, fishing, and photography of its famous sea stacks. Hike up the majestic sand dunes for a breathtaking view of the Pacific Ocean that stretches endlessly before you. Cape Kiwanda is the perfect spot for those who seek both relaxation and adventure in nature's arms.

Location: Cape Kiwanda State Natural Area, Pacific City, OR 97135, USA

Closest City or Town: Pacific City

How to Get There: Accessible via Pacific City on Cape Kiwanda Dr from US-101 S.

GPS Coordinates: 45.2328335° N, 123.9701863° W

Best Time to Visit: Late spring through early fall

Pass/Permit/Fees: Free access

Did You Know? Cape Kiwanda's unique sandstone formations are rapidly eroding; some features might be gone in a few years.

Website:
https://stateparks.oregon.gov/index.cfm?do=park.profile&parkId=130

PORT ORFORD

Prehistoric Gardens

Step back in time and experience a world ruled by dinosaurs at Prehistoric Gardens, nestled in the lush rainforest of the Oregon Coast. This unique outdoor park invites you to explore life-sized replicas of dinosaurs, each carefully crafted to offer a glimpse into the ancient past. Wander among the giants of the Mesozoic era, surrounded by the vibrant greenery that mirrors their once-native habitat. Located just off the scenic Highway 101 in Port Orford, this attraction combines education with enchantment, perfect for families and paleontology enthusiasts alike.

Location: 36848 US-101, Port Orford, OR 97465, USA

Closest City or Town: Port Orford, just a few minutes from the site

How to Get There: From downtown Port Orford, head north on US-101 for approximately 2.5 miles. Look for the sign on the right-hand side of the highway, which marks the entrance to Prehistoric Gardens.

GPS Coordinates: 42.6121232° N, 124.3929161° W

Best Time to Visit: The gardens are lush and most enjoyable in the spring and summer months, when the weather is mild and the foliage is at its peak.

Pass/Permit/Fees: Entry fees apply; please check the website for current pricing.

Did You Know? Prehistoric Gardens was established in 1955 and has been educating and delighting visitors with its blend of scientific accuracy and artistic interpretation ever since.

Website:

PORTLAND

International Rose Test Garden

Immerse yourself in a heavenly aroma at the International Rose Test Garden in Portland, where over 10,000 rose bushes of approximately 650 varieties paint a vivid palette of colors. Established during World War I, this garden serves as a testing ground for new rose varieties and as a sanctuary of peace. Stroll through the attractively laid-out walkways, admire the blooms, and partake in seasonal rose-themed events. It's a picturesque backdrop not only for garden lovers but for anyone wishing to behold nature in its most refined form.

Location: 400 SW Kingston Ave, Portland, OR 97205-5883

Closest City or Town: Portland

How to Get There: From downtown Portland, head southwest towards Washington Park via SW Park Pl.

GPS Coordinates: 45.5189524° N, 122.7052686° W

Best Time to Visit: Late spring to early summer when blooms are at their peak

Pass/Permit/Fees: Free admission

Did You Know? It's the oldest continuously operating public rose test garden in the United States.

Website:
https://www.portlandoregon.gov/parks/finder/index.cfm?action=viewpark&propertyid=1113

Powell's City of Books

Step into the literary world at Powell's City of Books, an iconic bookstore in Portland that spans a whole city block and stocks over a million books. As one of the largest independent bookstores in the world, Powell's offers an unparalleled selection of new, used, and out-of-print books that could captivate any bibliophile for hours. The color-coded rooms and knowledgeable staff help navigate this immense trove of literature, guaranteed to pull you into its labyrinth of stories.

Location: 1005 W Burnside St, Portland, OR 97209-3114

Closest City or Town: Portland

How to Get There: Located at the corner of Burnside St and 10th Ave in downtown Portland. Easily accessible by public transport or on foot in downtown.

GPS Coordinates: 45.5230928° N, 122.6812478° W

Best Time to Visit: Any time of year; rainy days offer a perfect excuse to get lost in a book.

Pass/Permit/Fees: Free access

Did You Know? Powell's once housed a technical bookstore visited by engineers from around the Pacific Northwest.

Website: http://www.powells.com/

Oregon Zoo: Together for Wildlife

Embark on a wild journey at the Oregon Zoo, located in Portland, where conservation meets education and entertainment. Home to over 2,600 animals from around the world, the zoo is a leader in wildlife preservation and scientific research. Wander through diverse ecosystems, attend educational talks, and meet the stars of the zoo: from majestic elephants to enigmatic snow leopards. The zoo's efforts in sustainability and wildlife conservation make it a beacon for animal lovers and environmental advocates alike.

Location: 4001 SW Canyon Rd, Portland, OR 97221-2799

Closest City or Town: Portland

How to Get There: Easily accessible from downtown Portland via US-26 W. Follow signs to the zoo within Washington Park.

GPS Coordinates: 45.5093572° N, 122.7142910° W

Best Time to Visit: Spring through fall for pleasant weather and active animals

Pass/Permit/Fees: Admission fee required, check website for current pricing

Did You Know? The Oregon Zoo was the first in America to host a community-based endangered species recovery project.

Website: http://www.oregonzoo.org/"

Pittock Mansion

Discover the grandeur of yesteryear at Pittock Mansion, a pristine beacon of Portland's historical landscape nestled high in the West Hills. Built in 1914 by Portland pioneers, Henry and Georgiana Pittock, this mansion offers breathtaking views of the city's skyline and the distant Cascade Mountains. Visitors can wander through beautifully preserved rooms that showcase early 20th-century elegance and learn about the city's transformation from a pioneer town to a bustling modern city.

Location: 3229 NW Pittock Dr, Portland, OR 97210-5099

Closest City or Town: Portland, Oregon

How to Get There: Accessible via US-26 W, take the exit toward Zoo/Forestry Center, follow signs for W Burnside St., then turn onto NW Barnes Rd and continue to Pittock Dr.

GPS Coordinates: 45.525185° N, 122.716694° W

Best Time to Visit: Spring and summer for the gardens in full bloom

Pass/Permit/Fees: Admission fee required, details on website

Did You Know? The mansion's unique architectural elements were sourced globally, reflecting the Pittock family's far-reaching influence.

Website: http://pittockmansion.org/

Lan Su Chinese Garden

Step into an authentic Chinese oasis in the heart of Portland at Lan Su Chinese Garden. Crafted by artisans from Suzhou, this garden is a window into Chinese culture and history, offering a tranquil escape with its winding paths, peaceful ponds, and exquisite pavilions. Engage with the garden's rich tapestry of flora, participate in traditional tea ceremonies, or attend one of the many cultural events that animate this space throughout the year.

Location: 239 NW Everett St, Portland, OR 97209-3957

Closest City or Town: Portland, Oregon

How to Get There: In downtown Portland, accessible via I-405 N, take exit 2B for Everett St, and continue to NW Everett St.

GPS Coordinates: 45.5256321° N, 122.6729955° W

Best Time to Visit: Spring for the blossoms or fall for the moon viewing festival

Pass/Permit/Fees: Admission fee required, details on website

Did You Know? The garden's lake is named 'Lake Zither', a homage to one of the traditional Chinese arts.

Website: http://www.lansugarden.org/

Oregon Museum of Science and Industry

Ignite your curiosity at the Oregon Museum of Science and Industry, a powerhouse of innovation located along the Willamette River. Dive into interactive science exhibits, view awe-inspiring planetarium shows, and board the historic submarine on site for a gripping glimpse into naval history. This museum offers a dynamic playground for minds of all ages, fostering a lifelong passion for learning and discovery.

Location: 1945 SE Water Ave, Portland, OR 97214-3356

Closest City or Town: Portland, Oregon

How to Get There: Easily reached from downtown Portland, head south on SE Martin Luther King Jr Blvd, then turn east onto SE Water Ave.

GPS Coordinates: 45.5083931° N, 122.6660355° W

Best Time to Visit: Year-round, with special events and exhibits changing seasonally

Pass/Permit/Fees: Admission fee required, details on website

Did You Know? OMSI possesses one of the few remaining operational WWII-era submarines, the USS Blueback.

Website: https://omsi.edu/

The Grotto National Sanctuary of Our Sorrowful Mother

Experience a spiritual oasis at The Grotto, a serene sanctuary offering 62 acres of beautifully landscaped gardens, walking paths, and peaceful reflection spaces. This Catholic shrine not only provides visitors with a tranquil retreat but also features impressive artworks, including sculptures and stained glass, that celebrate religious devotion. The highlight is the cliff-top meditation chapel, accessed via elevator, offering panoramic views of the lush surroundings.

Location: 8840 NE Skidmore, Portland, OR 97220

Closest City or Town: Portland, Oregon

How to Get There: North from downtown Portland, take I-205 N to NE Killingsworth St., follow signs to NE Skidmore St.

GPS Coordinates: 45.5532151° N, 122.5735354° W

Best Time to Visit: Early summer when the rhododendrons bloom

Pass/Permit/Fees: Entrance to the lower gardens is free; fee for elevator to upper gardens

Did You Know? The Grotto's elevator ascends 110 feet through solid basalt.

Website: http://thegrotto.org/

Portland Art Museum

Delve into a world of artistic wonder at the Portland Art Museum, one of the oldest museums in the Northwest. Explore an extensive collection that spans centuries and continents, from Native American artifacts to contemporary art installations. Special exhibitions often feature works from around the globe, making every visit a fresh encounter with the visual arts. The museum also hosts lectures, films, and family programs, enriching Portland's cultural life.

Location: 1219 SW Park Ave, Portland, OR 97205-2430

Closest City or Town: Portland, Oregon

How to Get There: Located in downtown Portland, accessible via SW Park Ave from any central city point.

GPS Coordinates: 45.5161500° N, 122.6833570° W

Best Time to Visit: All year, with rotating special exhibits

Pass/Permit/Fees: Admission fee required, free on the first Thursday of every month

Did You Know? The museum was founded in late 19th century and has grown to house over 42,000 pieces.

Website: https://portlandartmuseum.org/"

Pearl District

Discover the vibrant heartbeat of Portland in the Pearl District, an area celebrated for its rich blend of arts, culture, and shopping. Once a neglected warehouse district, it has transformed into a bustling urban enclave offering a mix of galleries, boutiques, and eateries. Wander through its charming streets to experience the innovative spirit and urban sophistication that make it a must-visit destination in the city.

Location: 404 NW 10th Ave # LL1, Portland, OR 97209-3184

Closest City or Town: Portland, Oregon

How to Get There: Easily accessible from anywhere in downtown Portland, the Pearl District is best reached by taking the Portland Streetcar to the NW 10th & Glisan stop, which places you in the heart of the district.

GPS Coordinates: 45.5259908° N, 122.6809012° W

Best Time to Visit: Year-round, with special events and gallery openings often happening during the First Thursday of each month.

Pass/Permit/Fees: No entrance fees, but parking and event fees may apply.

Did You Know? The Pearl District was largely industrial until the late 1990s when an urban renaissance began transforming it into one of Portland's most prestigious neighborhoods.

Website: http://pearlhelp.com/

Portland Saturday Market

Immerse yourself in the lively atmosphere of the Portland Saturday Market, a vibrant gathering space that celebrates the community's creative talents. Operating since 1974, this event showcases handmade arts and crafts, food from around the world, and live music, embodying Portland's eclectic spirit. Situated in the historic Old Town, it's the largest continuously operating outdoor arts and crafts market in the United States.

Location: 108 W Burnside St, Portland, OR 97209-4008

Closest City or Town: Portland, Oregon

How to Get There: The market is centrally located in downtown Portland, best reached via the MAX Light Rail to the Skidmore Fountain Station.

GPS Coordinates: 45.5226614° N, 122.6697468° W

Best Time to Visit: Open every weekend from March through Christmas Eve, with the most vibrant scene in summer.

Pass/Permit/Fees: Free entry, with products for purchase.

Did You Know? The market boasts over 350 small businesses and artisans, contributing significantly to the local economy.

Website: http://www.portlandsaturdaymarket.com/

Metropolitan Area Express (MAX)

Step aboard the Metropolitan Area Express, or MAX, Portland's pioneering light rail system that threads the city together. Connecting far-reaching neighborhoods from Gresham to Hillsboro through the scenic downtown corridor, MAX offers a green and efficient way to explore the city's diverse attractions—be it the cultural richness of Portland's downtown or the quiet charm of suburban areas.

Location: G76M+77 Portland, Oregon

Closest City or Town: Portland, Oregon

How to Get There: MAX lines are easily accessible throughout the Portland metropolitan area, with stations strategically located near major attractions and neighborhoods.

GPS Coordinates: 45.4967101° N, 122.7057971° W

Best Time to Visit: All year round; take advantage of Park & Ride locations for the most convenient experience.

Pass/Permit/Fees: Tickets are required for travel, with fares depending on travel zones. Day passes are also available.

Did You Know? MAX played a key role during the 1990 NBA Finals, carrying fans to and from the games efficiently, earning city-wide accolades.

Website: http://www.trimet.org/

South Waterfront Lower Tram Terminal

Ascend from the South Waterfront Lower Tram Terminal for panoramic views aboard the Portland Aerial Tram. This unique tram experience isn't just for commuters—it's an adventure offering unparalleled vistas of the cityscape and Mount Hood. Starting at the sleek and modern terminal, the journey to the upper level marries urban and natural beauty uniquely typical of Portland.

Location: 3303 S Bond Ave, Portland, OR 97239

Closest City or Town: Portland, Oregon

How to Get There: Located in the South Waterfront district, it is accessible via the Portland Streetcar to the SW Moody & Gibbs stop, only steps away from the terminal.

GPS Coordinates: 45.4992710° N, 122.6710100° W

Best Time to Visit: Open year-round, with clearer skies in summer offering the best views.

Pass/Permit/Fees: Small fee applies for round-trip tickets, with discounts for students and seniors.

Did You Know? The tram travels a distance of 3,300 feet horizontally and ascends 500 feet in elevation from bottom to top.

Website: http://gobytram.com/

Forest Park

Lose yourself in the vast wilderness of Forest Park, one of the largest urban forests in the United States. With over 80 miles of trails and lush woodland stretching over 5,200 acres, it's a paradise for hikers, bird watchers, and nature enthusiasts alike. The park's dense forests and extensive trails provide a serene escape from the urban excitement of nearby Portland, offering a natural refuge that feels worlds away.

Location: 8427 NW Skyline Blvd, Portland, OR 97229

Closest City or Town: Portland, Oregon

How to Get There: Access the park from NW 29th Ave and Upshur St, where you'll find trailhead and parking. Most trails are well-signposted.

GPS Coordinates: 45.6104712° N, 122.8193411° W

Best Time to Visit: Enjoyable year-round, but particularly magical in fall when the foliage changes color.

Pass/Permit/Fees: No entrance fee; parking at some trailheads may be charged.

Did You Know? Forest Park was established in 1948 and is home to more than 112 bird and 62 mammal species.

Website: http://www.forestparkconservancy.org/forest-park/"

Portland Japanese Garden

Step into a serene world at the Portland Japanese Garden, where tranquility meets natural beauty. Immerse yourself in a landscape of peaceful water features, koi-filled ponds, immaculate plant arrangements, and classic stone laneways. Nestled within Washington Park, this garden stands as a testament to the refined aesthetics of Japanese gardening and cultural authenticity.

Location: 611 SW Kingston Ave, Portland, OR 97205-5886

Closest City or Town: Portland, Oregon

How to Get There: Drive west from downtown Portland on US-26, take the exit toward the Oregon Zoo and follow signs to Washington Park. Portland Japanese Garden is well-signed within the park.

GPS Coordinates: 45.5188634° N, 122.7080354° W

Best Time to Visit: Spring for cherry blossoms or fall for vibrant foliage colors

Pass/Permit/Fees: Entry fee required; please visit the website for current rates

Did You Know? The garden was deemed the most beautiful and authentic Japanese garden outside of Japan by the former Ambassador of Japan to the U.S.

Website: http://japanesegarden.org/

Pioneer Courthouse Square

Discover the heart of Portland at Pioneer Courthouse Square, affectionately known as Portland's living room. This bustling public space hosts over 300 events a year, from farmers markets to cultural festivals, drawing both locals and tourists alike. Located in the core of downtown Portland, the square's distinctive brick patterns and welcoming steps offer a perfect vantage point for city life.

Location: 701 SW 6th Ave, Portland, OR 97204

Closest City or Town: Portland, Oregon

How to Get There: Located in downtown Portland, easily accessible by MAX Light Rail or by bus, disembark at Pioneer Square Station.

GPS Coordinates: 45.5172266° N, 122.6744653° W

Best Time to Visit: Year-round, with special events often held in summer

Pass/Permit/Fees: Free to the public

Did You Know? The square's design features 24,000 personalized bricks bought by community members in the early 1980s as a fundraising effort.

Website: http://thesquarepdx.org/

St. Johns Bridge

Marvel at the architectural splendor of the St. Johns Bridge, a stunning suspension bridge that spans the Willamette River. This iconic

Portland landmark, with its gothic-style towers and green hue, offers a picturesque crossing for vehicles and pedestrians alike. Running over the Cathedral Park, it provides an unmatched backdrop for photographers and sightseers.

Location: U.S. Highway 30, Portland, OR 97210

Closest City or Town: Portland, Oregon

How to Get There: Take U.S. Highway 30 west out of downtown Portland; the bridge and park are visible and accessible from the highway.

GPS Coordinates: 45.5564773° N, 122.7354037° W

Best Time to Visit: All year, particularly beautiful during sunrise and sunset

Pass/Permit/Fees: None

Did You Know? When opened in 1931, it was the longest suspension bridge west of the Mississippi River.

Website: https://www.portlandoregon.gov/inr_view.cfm?id=114

Tom McCall Waterfront Park

Energize your spirit at Tom McCall Waterfront Park, a vibrant stretch along the Willamette River in downtown Portland. Ideal for jogging, cycling, or simply enjoying a leisurely stroll, this park transforms into a hub of activity during festivals like the Oregon Brewers Festival and the Portland Rose Festival.

Location: Front Avenue, Portland, OR 97205

Closest City or Town: Portland, Oregon

How to Get There: The park is easily accessible from anywhere in downtown Portland, just head towards the river from any point.

GPS Coordinates: 45.5227536° N, 122.6699971° W

Best Time to Visit: Spring and summer for festivals and outdoor activities

Pass/Permit/Fees: Free to the public

Did You Know? The park was renamed in 1984 in honor of former Oregon Governor Tom McCall.

Website: http://www.portlandoregon.gov/parks/finder/index.cfm

Oregon Historical Society

Dive deep into the rich tapestry of Oregon's past at the Oregon Historical Society. Located in the heart of Portland's cultural district, this museum is brimming with artifacts, photographs, and exhibits that chronicle the state's storied history. From the Native American heritage to the pioneer days and beyond, each exhibit captivates and educates.

Location: 1200 SW Park Ave, Portland, OR 97205-2483

Closest City or Town: Portland, Oregon

How to Get There: Easily reached by public transport or on foot in downtown Portland, near the Portland Art Museum.

GPS Coordinates: 45.5159110° N, 122.6824320° W

Best Time to Visit: Any season, with special exhibitions throughout the year

Pass/Permit/Fees: Admission fee required, check website for details

Did You Know? The society holds one of the largest collections of state history materials in the U.S.

Website: http://www.ohs.org/"

Crystal Springs Rhododendron Garden

Discover a serene escape in the heart of Portland at Crystal Springs Rhododendron Garden, where natural beauty meets meticulous landscaping. Wander through blossoming rhododendrons and azaleas that create a spectacular palette of colors from bright pinks to deep purples. Situated near Reed College and Eastmoreland Golf Course, this garden is a tranquil haven for both plant enthusiasts and casual visitors alike. The enchanting water features and the diverse bird species that call this garden home add to the charm, providing a picturesque setting perfect for photography or peaceful contemplation.

Location: 5801 SE 28th Avenue, Portland, OR 97202

Closest City or Town: Portland, Oregon

How to Get There: Take SE Powell Blvd in Portland and turn south onto SE 28th Avenue. The garden entrance is just past Woodstock Blvd.

GPS Coordinates: 45.4799° N, 122.6355° W

Best Time to Visit: Spring is ideal when the rhododendrons are in full bloom.

Pass/Permit/Fees: Small entrance fee during bloom season; free admission during off-season.

Did You Know? This garden was initially started in 1950 by rhododendron enthusiasts and has grown to feature over 2,500 rhododendrons and azaleas.

Website: https://www.crystalspringsgardenpdx.org/

Hoyt Arboretum

Embark on a botanical journey at Hoyt Arboretum, located just a stone's throw from downtown Portland. This living museum boasts a collection of over 2,000 species of trees and plants from around the world, creating a lush tapestry of flora year-round. Trails meander through the arboretum, offering visitors a chance to explore different ecosystems and learn about global tree conservation. Unique for its extensive collection of conifers and maples, it serves as a vital resource for educational programs and a sanctuary for those seeking solace in nature.

Location: 4000 SW Fairview Blvd Fisherlane, Portland, OR 97221-2706

Closest City or Town: Portland, Oregon

How to Get There: Access is easiest from downtown Portland. Take SW Jefferson St to SW 18th Ave and follow signs to Washington Park, continuing to the arboretum.

GPS Coordinates: 45.5163° N, 122.7152° W

Best Time to Visit: Beautiful year-round, but especially vibrant in fall when the maples are changing colors.

Pass/Permit/Fees: Entry is free; some special events and programs may charge a fee.

Did You Know? Hoyt Arboretum is home to a rare dawn redwood, thought to be extinct until rediscovered in China in 1944.

Website: http://www.hoytarboretum.org/

Multnomah County Central Library

Step into the grandeur of the Multnomah County Central Library, not only a repository of knowledge but also a masterpiece of early 20th-century architecture. As the oldest library on the West Coast, established in 1913, it offers a voyage through time with its majestic Georgian-style structure and historic collections. Located in the vibrant heart of Portland, it remains a cornerstone for the community, providing vast resources and dynamic spaces that foster learning, creativity, and connection among its visitors.

Location: 801 SW 10th Ave, Portland, OR 97205-2520

Closest City or Town: Portland, Oregon

How to Get There: Located in downtown Portland, it is easily accessible by public transport or by driving down SW 10th Ave from Burnside St.

GPS Coordinates: 45.5191° N, 122.6832° W

Best Time to Visit: Open year-round; visit during off-peak hours for a quieter experience.

Pass/Permit/Fees: Free entry.

Did You Know? This library holds more than 17 miles of bookshelves and an impressive rare book collection that includes early manuscripts and original works.

Website: http://www.multcolib.org/agcy/cen.html

Mount Tabor Park

Explore the unique landscape of Mount Tabor Park, an extinct volcanic cinder cone right in the middle of Portland. This park not only offers panoramic views of the city and lush green spaces but also boasts a variety of recreational activities such as hiking, biking, and basketball. It's a favorite spot for both locals and visitors seeking a nature retreat without leaving the urban environment. The park's open reservoirs, historic structures, and winding pathways make it a perfect destination for a leisurely afternoon or a vigorous morning workout.

Location: SE 69th and Belmont Street, Portland, OR 97215

Closest City or Town: Portland, Oregon

How to Get There: Access the park from SE Belmont St, then head south on SE 69th Ave. Parking is available along SE 60th Ave and at the visitor center.

GPS Coordinates: 45.5149° N, 122.5950° W

Best Time to Visit: Enjoyable in all seasons; particularly lovely in the spring and summer.

Pass/Permit/Fees: No entrance fees.

Did You Know? Mount Tabor is one of the few volcanic cinder cones located within a city in the United States.

Website: http://portlandoregon.gov/parks/finder/index.cfm

REDMOND

Smith Rock State Park

Venture into the rugged landscapes of Smith Rock State Park, an internationally renowned climbing destination in Central Oregon. With majestic rock spires that tower above the Crooked River, the park is a climber's paradise, offering routes for all levels, from beginners to expert. Besides climbing, visitors can indulge in hiking, mountain biking, and wildlife viewing, especially golden eagles and prairie falcons. The dramatic vistas and the challenging Misery Ridge Trail attract adventurers and photographers alike, seeking to capture the awe-inspiring beauty of this natural wonder.

Location: 9V87+93 Terrebonne, Oregon

Closest City or Town: Redmond, Oregon

How to Get There: From Redmond, take US-97 N for about 6 miles until reaching the park entrance, marked by signage for Smith Rock State Park.

GPS Coordinates: 44.3682° N, 121.1406° W

Best Time to Visit: Spring and fall offer the most pleasant weather for climbing and hiking.

Pass/Permit/Fees: A day-use parking pass is required.

Did You Know? Smith Rock is often considered the birthplace of modern American sport climbing.

Website: http://oregonstateparks.org/index.cfm

REEDSPORT

Oregon Dunes National Recreation Area

Unleash your inner adventurer at Oregon Dunes National Recreation Area, where miles of wind-sculpted sand dunes offer a playground unlike any other. Located along the scenic coast of Oregon, these vast dunes provide a dramatic backdrop for a variety of high-energy activities. Turn the excitement up with dune buggy rides, or take a serene hike through the ever-changing sands. Don't miss the thrill of sandboarding down these natural giants—an experience unique to this picturesque location.

Location: 855 Highway Avenue, Reedsport, OR 97467

Closest City or Town: Reedsport, Oregon

How to Get There: From Reedsport, head north on US-101 for about 5 miles, then turn right onto E Beach Loop Rd. Follow the signs to the designated parking areas.

GPS Coordinates: 43.7035323° N, 124.1059618° W

Best Time to Visit: Summer for the best weather, but early spring and late fall offer less crowded conditions.

Pass/Permit/Fees: Day-use fees apply; check the website for up-to-date information.

Did You Know? The Oregon Dunes span approximately 40 miles along the coast, making them one of the largest expanses of temperate coastal sand dunes in the world.

Website:
https://www.fs.usda.gov/recarea/siuslaw/recreation/recarea/?reci d=42465

RIM DR

Rim Drive

Circle the wonders of Crater Lake along Rim Drive, a route that offers awe-inspiring views of one of the deepest lakes in the United States. Each twist and turn of this 33-mile drive around Crater Lake presents photo-worthy panoramas and numerous overlooks to stop and soak in the natural beauty. Ideal for leisurely drives or invigorating bicycle rides, Rim Drive encapsulates the essence of this volcanic wonderland.

Location: Rim Dr, Oregon, USA

Closest City or Town: Klamath Falls, Oregon

How to Get There: From Klamath Falls, head northwest on OR-62 W. Follow signs for Crater Lake National Park and Rim Drive.

GPS Coordinates: 42.9127833° N, 122.0722417° W

Best Time to Visit: Late June to October when the entire drive is typically free from snow.

Pass/Permit/Fees: Entrance fee to Crater Lake National Park applies.

Did You Know? Rim Drive features over 30 scenic pullouts, offering different perspectives and photographic opportunities of Crater Lake's vibrant blue waters.

Website:https://www.nps.gov/crla/planyourvisit/scenic-rim-drive.htm

RIM VILLAGE

Crater Lake National Park

Experience the deep blue tranquility of Crater Lake National Park, home to the deepest lake in the United States, formed by the collapse of Mount Mazama. This caldera lake is renowned for its stunning clarity and striking color. Explore the park's numerous hiking trails, witness spectacular views from Watchman Overlook, or take a boat tour to Wizard Island during your visit. The park's unique geological features make it a must-visit destination for nature lovers and geology enthusiasts alike.

Location: Crater Lake National Park, 570 Rim Village Dr, Oregon 97604

Closest City or Town: Klamath Falls, Oregon

How to Get There: Drive north from Klamath Falls on OR-97, then take OR-62 west to the park.

GPS Coordinates: 42.9098571° N, 122.1409236° W

Best Time to Visit: Summer for full access to all park facilities; winter for snowshoeing and cross-country skiing.

Pass/Permit/Fees: National park entrance fees apply.

Did You Know? Crater Lake is often considered the cleanest and clearest large body of water in the world.

Website: https://www.nps.gov/crla/index.htm

SALEM

Willamette Valley

Savor the flavors of the Pacific Northwest in Willamette Valley, a verdant expanse renowned for its award-winning vineyards and rustic charm. This fertile region not only produces some of the best Pinot Noir in the world but also offers a cornucopia of artisanal foods and craft beverages. A visit here is not just a journey for your palette but also a delightful exploration through charming towns, historic sites, and lush countryside.

Location: Oregon, USA

Closest City or Town: Salem, Oregon

How to Get There: Easily accessible from I-5, which runs through the heart of the valley.

GPS Coordinates: 44.9425540° N, 122.9337615° W

Best Time to Visit: Late spring through fall for the best wine-tasting experience and beautiful foliage.

Pass/Permit/Fees: No entrance fees for the valley; winery tasting fees vary.

Did You Know? The Willamette Valley is known as one of the premier Pinot Noir producing areas in the world, thanks to its ideal climate and soil conditions.

Website:https://www.nwp.usace.army.mil/Locations/Willamette-Valley/

Enchanted Forest Theme Park

Step into a world of whimsy at the Enchanted Forest Theme Park, a magical destination in Salem, Oregon, that captivates visitors with its blend of fairy-tale charm and thrilling rides. Whether wandering through Storybook Lane, experiencing the adrenaline rush of the Ice Mountain Bobsleds, or enjoying live entertainment, the park offers enchanting experiences for all ages. Create unforgettable memories in this quirky, family-owned amusement park where fantasy comes to life.

Location: 8462 Enchanted Way SE, Salem, OR 97392-9444

Closest City or Town: Salem, Oregon

How to Get There: From Salem, take I-5 S to Exit 248. Follow signs to Enchanted Way SE.

GPS Coordinates: 44.8314606° N, 123.0084450° W

Best Time to Visit: Spring through fall for the best weather and full park access.

Pass/Permit/Fees: Admission fees apply; check the website for details.

Did You Know? Opened in 1971, Enchanted Forest Theme Park was hand-built by Roger Tofte, who transformed the wooded land into a beloved Oregon attraction.

Website: http://www.enchantedforest.com/

Salem's Riverfront Carousel

Let your childhood memories take flight at Salem's Riverfront Carousel, where handcrafted horses and magical chariots spin gracefully along the Willamette River. This enchanting carousel, bustling with colorful artistry and nostalgic music, offers a delightful experience for all ages. Located in the heart of Salem's scenic Riverfront Park, it's the perfect blend of art and tradition, creating delightful moments under the Oregon sky. Whether reliving your childhood or creating new memories, this carousel promises a whimsical ride through time.

Location: 101 Front St NE, Salem, OR 97301-3473

Closest City or Town: Salem, Oregon

How to Get There: From I-5, take exit 253 for OR-22 toward the city center. Continue on OR-22, which becomes Mission St NE. Turn left onto Liberty St NE and then right onto Division St NE to reach the park.

GPS Coordinates: 44.9410879° N, 123.0430662° W

Best Time to Visit: Spring through fall when the weather allows for a pleasant outdoor experience.

Pass/Permit/Fees: Free to visit, with a nominal charge for carousel rides.

Did You Know? Each horse on the carousel has a unique name and design, meticulously crafted by local artisans.

Website: http://www.salemcarousel.org/

Oregon State Capitol

Explore the heart of Oregon's governance at the Oregon State Capitol, located in Salem. This modern public building, adorned with the iconic Oregon Pioneer statue atop its dome, offers guided tours that delve into the state's legislative history. Stroll through the art deco interior, learn about Oregon's unique legislative processes, and enjoy the beautifully landscaped gardens. The capitol steps provide a panoramic view of the bustling city against a backdrop of the picturesque Willamette Valley.

Location: 900 Court St NE, Salem, OR 97301-4042

Closest City or Town: Salem, Oregon

How to Get There: Located downtown, the capitol is easily accessible from I-5. Take exit 253 for OR-22/ Mission St toward the city center and follow signs to the state capitol.

GPS Coordinates: 44.9384539° N, 123.0303428° W

Best Time to Visit: Year-round, with legislative sessions providing a unique insight during spring months.

Pass/Permit/Fees: No entrance fees; tours are free of charge.

Did You Know? The building is the third capitol in Salem, with the previous two destroyed by fire.

Website: http://www.oregoncapitol.com/

SEASIDE

Seaside Aquarium

Uncover the mysteries of marine life at Seaside Aquarium, one of the oldest aquariums on the West Coast. This compact yet fascinating aquarium invites you to interact with native marine species through touch tanks and informative displays. Whether it's feeding the playful seals or learning about coastal ecosystems, this family-friendly destination adds a splash of educational fun to any visit to Seaside. Located just steps from the ocean, it's a gateway to understanding the creatures of the Pacific Northwest.

Location: 200 North Prom, Seaside, OR 97138-5945

Closest City or Town: Seaside, Oregon

How to Get There: Follow Hwy 101 to Seaside and turn onto 1st Ave towards the Promenade. The aquarium is centrally located along the beachfront.

GPS Coordinates: 45.9951560° N, 123.9294695° W

Best Time to Visit: Open year-round, but summer offers additional educational programs.

Pass/Permit/Fees: Admission fee required for entry.

Did You Know? Seaside Aquarium was instrumental in initiating the program that helped save the Northern Elephant Seals from extinction.

Website: http://www.seasideaquarium.com/index.php

Turnaround at Seaside

Capture panoramic ocean views at the Turnaround at Seaside, a historic and symbolic site marking the end of the Lewis and Clark Trail. This spot is not only a tribute to American exploration but also a vibrant focal point of Seaside. Stroll along the broad promenade, enjoy the soothing sounds of the Pacific, or simply soak in the dramatic sunsets. With its sculptures commemorating the historic expedition and unbeatable ocean vistas, the Turnaround offers a picture-perfect backdrop for an Oregon coast adventure.

Location: 30 N Prom, Seaside, OR 97138-5823

Closest City or Town: Seaside, Oregon

How to Get There: Located at the end of Broadway Street where it meets the ocean, easily reachable from Hwy 101 by following signs to the city center.

GPS Coordinates: 45.9935056° N, 123.9290486° W

Best Time to Visit: Year-round, with summer providing lively beachfront activities.

Pass/Permit/Fees: No entrance fees; public access.

Did You Know? The Turnaround is one of the most photographed spots on the Oregon Coast, capturing the spirit of both history and natural beauty.

Website: http://www.lewisandclarktrail.com/section4/orcities/seaside/endoft hetrail.htm

Camp 18 Logging Museum

Step back in time at Camp 18 Logging Museum, where Oregon's rich logging history is preserved in a sprawling outdoor museum. Nestled in the lush forests near Seaside, this museum features a collection of vintage logging equipment and rustic log buildings. Dive into the life of loggers through interactive exhibits and the aroma of fresh-cut timber. The restaurant on site serves hearty meals, complemented by the cozy ambiance of a massive stone fireplace, making it a unique culinary and historical experience in one.

Location: 42364 Sunset Highway, Seaside, OR 97138-6162

Closest City or Town: Seaside, Oregon

How to Get There: Take Hwy 26 west from Portland towards Seaside. Camp 18 is visibly located on the highway, marked by large logging equipment on display.

GPS Coordinates: 45.8851971° N, 123.6139468° W

Best Time to Visit: Open year-round, but particularly inviting in fall when the surrounding forests are a tapestry of colors.

Pass/Permit/Fees: Free entry; donations are appreciated.

Did You Know? The entire museum is crafted from materials salvaged from old logging and mill operations.

Website: https://www.orartswatch.org/camp-18-a-walk-through-history-in-logs/"

Seaside Beach

Uncover the quintessential Oregon coast experience at Seaside Beach, where the endless stretches of sandy shores invite you to relax, play, and explore. Nestled on the northern Oregon Coast, Seaside Beach offers a picturesque escape with its gentle waves and iconic promenade lined with shops and cafes. Whether it's building sandcastles, enjoying seaside rides, or just strolling by the calming waves, there is something for everyone at this vibrant coastal retreat.

Location: 229-299 S Promenade, Seaside, OR 97138, USA

Closest City or Town: Seaside, Oregon

How to Get There: Access Seaside Beach by heading north on Hwy 101, turning west on Broadway St., which leads directly to the Promenade.

GPS Coordinates: 45.9931529° N, 123.9308760° W

Best Time to Visit: Summer for best weather, though early fall often offers pleasant days with fewer crowds.

Pass/Permit/Fees: None required for beach access.

Did You Know? Seaside Beach is famed for its annual volleyball tournament, one of the largest amateur events of its kind in the United States.

Website: https://visittheoregoncoast.com/cities/seaside/

SILVERTON

The Oregon Garden

Step into a living canvas at The Oregon Garden, where 80 acres of botanical landscapes offer an awe-inspiring testament to the diversity of nature. Located in Silverton, just east of Salem, this beautifully designed garden features themed sections including conifer, rose, and water gardens. Visitors can explore a world of flora through guided tours or at their own pace, finding seasonal colors and educational opportunities at every turn.

Location: 879 W Main St, Silverton, OR 97381-2243

Closest City or Town: Silverton, Oregon

How to Get There: Drive east from Salem on Silverton Rd NE, which becomes Main St as you enter Silverton, leading you directly to the garden.

GPS Coordinates: 44.9950179° N, 122.7885873° W

Best Time to Visit: Spring through fall for the best floral displays.

Pass/Permit/Fees: Admission fees apply; check the website for current pricing and membership options.

Did You Know? The Oregon Garden is home to a Frank Lloyd Wright-designed house, which was moved and restored on this site to preserve its history.

Website: http://www.oregongarden.org/

SISTERS

Sahalie and Koosah Falls

Experience the awe of Oregon's natural beauty at Sahalie and Koosah Falls, located along the McKenzie River trail. These powerful cascades plunge into azure pools below, surrounded by ancient forests that enhance the area's mystical feel. Hiking the easy trail linking both falls offers not just exquisite views but also a refreshing encounter with nature's raw power and tranquility.

Location: Highway 126, Sisters, OR 97759

Closest City or Town: Sisters, Oregon

How to Get There: From Sisters, take Hwy 126 east for approximately 20 miles. Well-signed parking areas for both falls are available along the highway.

GPS Coordinates: 44.1332117° N, 122.4842791° W

Best Time to Visit: Late spring and early summer when the water flow is at its peak.

Pass/Permit/Fees: No fees required.

Did You Know? The names Sahalie and Koosah come from the Chinook language, meaning '"heaven"' and '"sky,"' respectively.

Website: http://www.oregon.com/recreation/sahalie-falls

THE DALLES

Columbia Gorge Discovery Center & Museum

Embark on a journey through time and nature at the Columbia Gorge Discovery Center & Museum, located at the gateway to the scenic Columbia River Gorge. This interactive museum offers a fascinating glimpse into the geological and cultural history of the area. Visitors can engage with exhibits on the Ice Age floods, native peoples, and the pioneering days of the Oregon Trail, all set against the breathtaking backdrop of the river itself.

Location: 5000 Discovery Dr, The Dalles, OR 97058-9755

Closest City or Town: The Dalles, Oregon

How to Get There: From downtown The Dalles, take W 6th St to Webber St, continue on Discovery Dr to the museum.

GPS Coordinates: 45.6544055° N, 121.2104392° W

Best Time to Visit: Year-round, with special events and exhibits featured seasonally.

Pass/Permit/Fees: Entrance fees apply; check the website for details.

Did You Know? The museum is located on a 54-acre site that includes 12 acres of native plants and wetlands, representing the gorge's natural ecosystem.

Website: http://www.gorgediscovery.org/

TILLAMOOK

Cape Meares Lighthouse

Discover panoramic ocean views and a slice of Oregon's maritime history at Cape Meares Lighthouse. Perched on a cliff on the Three Capes Scenic Route, this charming lighthouse dates back to 1890. Visitors can tour the lighthouse, explore the surrounding old growth forest in Cape Meares State Scenic Viewpoint, and possibly spot migrating whales from the coastline.

Location: 3500 Cape Meares Loop, Tillamook, OR 97141

Closest City or Town: Tillamook, Oregon

How to Get There: From Tillamook, take OR-131 N (Netarts Hwy W) to First St., follow signs to Cape Meares Loop and the lighthouse.

GPS Coordinates: 45.4731170° N, 123.9686662° W

Best Time to Visit: Spring for whale watching and less crowded tours.

Pass/Permit/Fees: No entrance fee; donations are accepted for lighthouse maintenance.

Did You Know? Cape Meares Lighthouse features the only Fresnel lens of its type on the Oregon coast, originally crafted in Paris in 1888.

Website: https://friendsofcapemeareslighthouse.com/

Tillamook Air Museum

Step into the grandeur of aviation history at the Tillamook Air Museum, housed in a massive World War II blimp hangar one of the largest wooden structures in the world. Immerse yourself in a collection of meticulously restored aircraft, where history takes flight right before your eyes. Located in scenic Tillamook, this museum is not just for aviation enthusiasts but for anyone fascinated by the ingenuity of aerial warfare and peacetime aviation alike.

Location: 6030 Hangar Rd, Tillamook, OR 97141-9641

Closest City or Town: Tillamook, Oregon

How to Get There: From downtown Tillamook, head north on US-101 N. Turn right onto Long Prairie Rd and follow the signs to the air museum.

GPS Coordinates: 45.4207296° N, 123.8035965° W

Best Time to Visit: Open year-round, but summer offers additional special events.

Pass/Permit/Fees: Admission fees apply. Check the website for current pricing.

Did You Know? The hangar was originally constructed to house blimps for anti-submarine patrol during WWII.

Website: http://www.tillamookair.com/

Cape Lookout State Park

Find your adventure at Cape Lookout State Park, a haven for hikers, campers, and nature lovers. With its breathtaking cliffside views of the Pacific Ocean, this park offers a plethora of outdoor activities from serene beachcombing to challenging treks along the Cape Trail. Whether you're looking to spot migrating whales or just want to escape into a coastal wonderland, Cape Lookout provides an unforgettable natural retreat.

Location: 928J+9G Tillamook, Oregon

Closest City or Town: Tillamook, Oregon

How to Get There: Take US-101 to the Three Capes Scenic Drive, following signs for Cape Lookout State Park.

GPS Coordinates: 45.3558220° N, 123.9714861° W

Best Time to Visit: Spring through fall for the best weather and whale watching opportunities.

Pass/Permit/Fees: Parking fee required; check the website for details.

Did You Know? The park is part of the migratory route for gray whales.

Website: http://oregonstateparks.org/index.cfm?do=parkPage.dsp_parkPage&parkId=134

TURNER

Willamette Valley Vineyards

Savor the taste of Oregon's famed Pinot noir at Willamette Valley Vineyards. Set in the rich landscapes of the Willamette Valley, this vineyard offers an exceptional journey through upscale wine tasting rooms and guided vineyard tours. Discover the delicate varietals that flourish in this region, enjoy food pairings, and relax on the terrace overlooking rows of vines stretching into the horizon.

Location: 8800 Enchanted Way SE, Turner, OR 97392-9580

Closest City or Town: Salem, Oregon

How to Get There: From Salem, take I-5 S to exit 248 for Turner. Continue on Enchanted Way SE directly into the vineyards.

GPS Coordinates: 44.8277935° N, 123.0123465° W

Best Time to Visit: Late spring to early fall for vineyard tours and wine tastings.

Pass/Permit/Fees: Tasting fees apply; check the website for details.

Did You Know? The Willamette Valley is internationally recognized as one of the premier Pinot noir producing areas.

Website: http://www.wvv.com/

WINSTON

Wildlife Safari

Embark on a thrilling expedition at Wildlife Safari, where you can drive through natural habitats filled with exotic animals from around the world. Situated in the picturesque town of Winston, Oregon, this drive-through safari lets you get up-close encounters with giraffes, rhinos, lions, and more. Each visit promises a new adventure, complete with interactive encounters and educational exhibits—perfect for family outings and wildlife enthusiasts alike.

Location: 1790 Safari Rd, Winston, OR 97496-8610

Closest City or Town: Roseburg, Oregon

How to Get There: Take I-5 S from Roseburg, then take exit 119 for Winston. Follow OR-42 and turn right onto Safari Rd.

GPS Coordinates: 43.1408081° N, 123.4274292° W

Best Time to Visit: Open year-round, with spring and fall providing the most comfortable weather for animal viewing.

Pass/Permit/Fees: Entrance fees apply; check the website for specifics.

Did You Know? Wildlife Safari is one of the few places in the U.S. where you can still see cheetahs running at full speed in a natural setting.

Website: http://www.wildlifesafari.net/"

WOODBURN

Woodburn Premium Outlets

Unleash your shopping spirit at Woodburn Premium Outlets, where fashion meets affordability in the heart of Oregon. With over 110 stores offering brands like Nike, Adidas, and The North Face at discounted prices, it's a paradise for bargain hunters and fashionistas alike. Nestled conveniently off I-5 in Woodburn, this outdoor shopping haven provides a pleasant stroll amidst a collection of shops offering something for everyone, from designer apparel to footwear and home goods.

Location: 1001 N Arney Rd, Woodburn, OR 97071

Closest City or Town: Woodburn, Oregon

How to Get There: From Portland, follow I-5 S to exit 271, then take a right onto Newberg Hwy, followed by a left onto Arney Road to reach the outlets.

GPS Coordinates: 45.1561674° N, 122.8785613° W

Best Time to Visit: weekdays to avoid crowds, especially during sales events

Pass/Permit/Fees: Free entry, parking available on site

Did You Know? The center hosts an annual tulip festival each spring that draws visitors from across the Pacific Northwest.

Website: http://www.premiumoutlets.com/outlet/woodburn

Wooden Shoe Tulip Farm

Immerse yourself in a colorful spectacle at Wooden Shoe Tulip Farm. Spanning over 40 acres, the farm explodes with vibrant tulips each spring, creating a photographer's dream landscape. Located in Woodburn, this family-owned farm not only offers stunning flower fields but also wine tasting, seasonal events, and a cozy gift shop filled with handmade goods. It's a perfect family getaway that promises peaceful walks and unforgettable memories among the blooms.

Location: 33814 S Meridian Rd, Woodburn, OR 97071-8773

Closest City or Town: Woodburn, Oregon

How to Get There: Take I-5 S from Portland, exit 271 for Woodburn, and follow signs south to Meridian Road.

GPS Coordinates: 45.1185107° N, 122.7489037° W

Best Time to Visit: Spring (March to April) during the Tulip Fest

Pass/Permit/Fees: Entry fees vary by season; check the website for details.

Did You Know? The farm's Tulip Fest features a 5K run through the tulip fields, adding a healthy twist to flower viewing.

Website: http://www.woodenshoe.com/

YACHATS

Yachats Coastline

Rediscover the wild, untouched beauty of the Pacific Northwest along the Yachats Coastline. With its dramatic vistas, crashing waves, and rocky shores, this stretch of the Oregon coast is a haven for nature lovers and photographers. Located along Highway 101 in Yachats, this rugged landscape offers numerous trails, tide pools, and panoramic views that make it a perfect spot for hiking, picnicking, or simply soaking in the ocean's timeless rhythms.

Location: 241 Highway 101 N, Yachats, OR 97498-9559

Closest City or Town: Yachats, Oregon

How to Get There: Drive along Highway 101, which runs directly through Yachats; the coastline is accessible via multiple points along the highway.

GPS Coordinates: 44.3112493° N, 124.1042883° W

Best Time to Visit: Summer for the best weather, winter for dramatic storm-watching

Pass/Permit/Fees: No fees for access; public areas are free.

Did You Know? Yachats is derived from the Chinook Word 'Yahuts,' meaning dark waters at the foot of the mountain.

Website: http://www.fs.usda.gov/recarea/siuslaw/recarea/

Devil's Churn

Venture to the awe-inspiring Devil's Churn, a narrow inlet carved by the relentless force of the sea. This stunning natural wonder, located south of Yachats, showcases the power and beauty of the Pacific Ocean as waves crash into the basalt chasm, producing dramatic spouts and roars. Ideal for those seeking a thrilling sight, the Churn offers an accessible trail leading to viewpoints where the ocean's might can be witnessed up close.

Location: Devils Churn, Oregon, USA

Closest City or Town: Yachats, Oregon

How to Get There: From Yachats, travel south on Highway 101 for about 16 miles, then follow the signs to the Devil's Churn parking area.

GPS Coordinates: 44.2841664° N, 124.1116282° W

Best Time to Visit: Spring through early fall for accessible trails and mild weather

Pass/Permit/Fees: A Northwest Forest Pass may be required; check local regulations.

Did You Know? Devil's Churn is thought to be over thousands of years old, a testament to the shaping forces of nature.

Website: https://en.wikipedia.org/wiki/Devils_Churn"

MAP

We have devised an interactive map that includes all destinations described in the book.

Upon scanning a provided QR code, a link will be sent to your email, allowing you access to this unique digital feature.

This map is both detailed and user-friendly, marking every location described within the pages of the book. It provides accurate addresses and GPS coordinates for each location, coupled with direct links to the websites of these stunning destinations.

Once you receive your email link and access the interactive map, you'll have an immediate and comprehensive overview of each site's location. This invaluable tool simplifies trip planning and navigation, making it a crucial asset for both first-time visitors and seasoned explorers of Washington.

Scan the following QR or type in the provided link to receive it:

https://jo.my/oregonbucketlistbonus

You will receive an email with links to access the Interactive Map. If you do not see our email, please look for it in spam or another section of your inbox.

In case you have any problems, you can write us at
TravelBucketList@becrepress.com

Made in United States
Troutdale, OR
12/16/2024

26765776R00070